Sawdust Trails in the Truckee Basin

A History of Lumbering Operations

Nevada County Historical Society Publications

A History of the Empire Mine
Charles A. Bohakel
A History of the North Star Mines:
Grass Valley, California 1851–1929
Marian F. Conway
Nuggets of Nevada County History
Juanita Kennedy Browne
Sketches of Yesterday and Today in Nevada County
Marilyn Starkey and Juanita Kennedy Browne
Sawdust Trails in the Truckee Basin:
A History of Lumbering Operations 1856–1936
Dick Wilson
A Tale of Two Cities and a Train:
History of the Nevada County Narrow Gauge Railroad 1874–1942
Juanita Kennedy Browne

Sawdust Trails in the Truckee Basin

A History of Lumbering Operations 1856–1936

Dick Wilson

NEVADA COUNTY HISTORICAL SOCIETY
Nevada City, California

Copyright © 1992 Richard Clayton Wilson
All rights reserved
Published by the Nevada County Historical Society
P.O. Box 1300, Nevada City, CA 95959

Maps, design, composition, and production by
Dave Comstock

Library of Congress Cataloging-in-Publication Data
Wilson, Dick, 1910–
Sawdust trails in the Truckee Basin : a history of lumbering
operations, 1856–1936 / Dick Wilson.
p.   cm.
Includes bibliographical references and index.
ISBN 0-915641-04-6
1. Lumbering—Truckee River Watershed (Calif. and Nev.)—History.
2. Logging—Truckee River Watershed (Calif. and Nev.)—History.
3. Truckee River Watershed (Calif. and Nev.)—History.   I. Title.
TS806.C3W55   1992
634.9′8′097943—dc20   91–34500
                                                     CIP

Contents

Acknowledgments	*vii*
Foreword	*ix*
Maps	*x–xiii*
1. Whittling on the Timberlands	1
2. Comstock Discovery Triggers Lumbering Boom	2
3. The Emerging Development Pattern, and the Men Who Shaped It	8
4. Lumbering Prospers as Mining Slumps	11
5. Animal Logging in the 1860s, Variety in the Mills	11
6. Rivers of Wood	15
7. Evolution of Log Chutes	21
8. Prime Timber, Cheap Stumpage	25
9. The Booming Seventies and Eighties	29
10. Variations in Logging	37
11. Icy Millponds and Cutover Pastures	45
12. Consolidation and Winding Down	48
13. Steam in the Woods	51
14. Fire in the Slash, at the Mills	56
15. Pulping the Fir	59
16. Axing the Virgin Remnants	59
Appendix: Lumbering Operations in the Truckee Basin	65
Sources Cited	84
Index	87

Illustrations

1. Sugar pine forest.	xiv
2. Water-powered upright saw.	3
3. Steam-powered circular saw.	4
4. Mules carrying cordwood.	7
5. Mill crew.	9
6. Kitchen crew.	10
7. Ox team pulling log wagons.	12
8. McGiffert log loader.	13
9. Gin pole log loader.	14
10. Spooner Station in 1880.	16

11. Spooner Station ca. 1940.   17
12. Spooner Station ca. 1985.   17
13. Clear Creek flume.   18
14. Clear Creek flume and lumber yard.   19
15. Donkey engine chute and spool post.   20
16. Donkey engine chute and bull block post.   21
17. Donkey engine chute.   22
18. Horse chute.   23
19. Logs arriving by horse chute.   24
20. W. H. Kruger.   28
21. Kruger's general store.   28
22. Alder Creek mill.   31
23. Verdi Lumber Company mill.   32
24. Box factory and kiln at Hobart Mills.   34
25. Hotel at Hobart Mills.   35
26. Stage depot at Hobart Mills.   35
27. Hobart Mills manager's house.   36
28. Log drive on Little Truckee River.   38
29. Carson & Tahoe Lumber Company mill at Glenbrook.   40
30. Incline mill and cable-rail line.   42
31. Steam wagon on log rails.   44
32. Doan three-wheeled steam wagon.   46
33. Steam wagon and trailers at Hobart Mills.   47
34. S. H. Marlette.   50
35. J. B. Overton.   51
36. Dolbeer donkey engine.   52
37. Bull donkey engine.   53
38. Locomotives at Hobart Mills.   55
39. Wood yard at Floriston.   58
40. Sixty-year-old stumps on Carson Range.   61
41. Stump pasture on Mount Rose.   62
42. William W. Bliss at Glenbrook mill site.   63
43. Abandoned mill pond near Verdi.   63
44. George D. Oliver.   64

Maps

1. Truckee River Basin headwaters.   x
2. Northwest Truckee River Basin headwaters.   xi
3. Northeast Truckee River Basin headwaters.   xii
4. South Truckee River Basin headwaters.   xiii

Acknowledgments

*H*alf a century ago the U.S. Forest Service sponsored a bibliographic research project performed by the WPA to abstract records of fires and lumbering in California and Western Nevada. The research was supplemental to forest surveys directed by A. E. Wieslander of the California (now the Pacific Southwest) Forest & Range Experiment Station. Highlights of the abstracts on lumbering the Truckee Basin were reported by Constance Knowles, supervising librarian on the WPA project. Her report proved to be a very useful reference.[1]

The abstracts on lumbering and fires are filed in the forestry library of the University of California, Berkeley. I am deeply indebted to Peter Evans, forestry librarian, for expediting my study of those materials which comprise a major basis for this publication.

My thanks are also extended to a number of individuals in the Forest Service for suggestions and reference materials. These include Dennis Galvin, librarian, Pacific Southwest Forest & Range Experiment Station, and the following Forest Service archaeologists: Linda Lux; Dick Markley, Dana Supernowics, Kathy Hardy, Anne Carlson and Penny Rucks.

My thanks are extended to the following for pertinent information (among any others overlooked in the listing, to whom I apologize): Susan Antipa, Librarian, Truckee Public Library; John Curtis, past president, Truckee Donner Historical Society; John Corbett, Truckee Donner Utility District; Stephen Wee, Jackson Research Projects, Davis, California; Ed Tyson, Searls Historical Library, Nevada City; Myron Hall, Consulting Forester, Citrus Heights, California; Thomas Macauley, Reno; Robert Blesse, Head, Special Collections Department, University of Nevada Library, Reno; Miriam Biro, North Lake Tahoe Museum, Tahoe City; Susan Evans,

1. Constance D. Knowles, *A History of Lumbering in the Truckee Basin from 1856 to 1936*. Office Report of California Forest and Range Experiment Station, U.S. Forest Service, Berkeley, 1942.

Curator, Lake Tahoe Historical Association; Robert Nyland, Railroad Museum, Carson City; John Fulton, Tahoe City; Gayle Kromydas, Donner State Park; William W. Bliss, Glenbrook; Mrs. Shelly Turner, Manager of Glenbrook Properties; Joe Mosconi, Verdi; Warren W. Richardson, Reno; William Dunbar, Rio Vista, California; Hobart Leonard, Nevada City; Arthur Koerber, Incline Village, Nevada; and Cheryl Oakes, Librarian, Forest History Society, Durham, NC.

Greatly appreciated was the access to files furnished by staffs of county recorders at Downieville, Nevada City, Placerville, Auburn, Reno, Carson City, and Minden. Staffs at the following offices were also very helpful: The Nevada Historical Society, Reno, and the Nevada State Library, Carson City.

Particularly appreciated was help from Professor William Rowley, University of Nevada History Department, for references and contacts and for suggestions on presentation of research results.

I'm most deeply indebted to David Comstock of Grass Valley, California, for expert advice on preparing this study for publication, and for making the maps so essential to its presentation.

My wife Dorothy merits special thanks for patient translation and conversion of my rough draft into something more readable.

R. C. "Dick" Wilson

Foreword

*I*n the mid-nineteenth century the Comstock silver strike generated pressure for a timber harvest of historic proportions, and to meet the demands for wood by Nevada miners, an army of loggers invaded the virgin forests of the nearby Truckee Basin. Scores of sawmills sprang up, and soon virtually every timbered canyon in the basin reverberated with axe strokes and whining headsaws.

Following that initial surge, it took three-quarters of a century of continuous lumbering before all but remnants of the vast Truckee forests were reduced to stumps and sawdust. During that period an estimated seven billion feet of sawtimber and ten million cords of fuel wood were harvested from those timberlands.[2] Enough wood, if all had been converted to planks and slabs four inches thick, to build a boardwalk thirty feet wide around the earth.

That harvest of wood provided square sets to line the stopes of Nevada mines, cordwood to feed the furnaces of Comstock stamp mills, sleepers to bed down hundreds of miles of the Central Pacific Railroad, fuel to stoke its locomotives, and building materials for many cities and farms in the treeless expanses of the West.

The material that follows, by text and illustrations, portrays the sequences of lumbering methods in the Truckee Basin and records the actions of the men who shaped the pattern of that history.

2. Combined estimates of timber volume cut by 1881 and timber volume standing at that date, as published in the *Reno Gazette*, September 14, 1881. That estimated total volume (of sawtimber plus cordwood) was evidently based on the judgments of local lumbermen and timber cruisers. Here, as throughout this report, sawtimber volumes are measured in board feet. A board foot is a unit of measure equal to the cubic contents of a board one foot square and one inch thick.

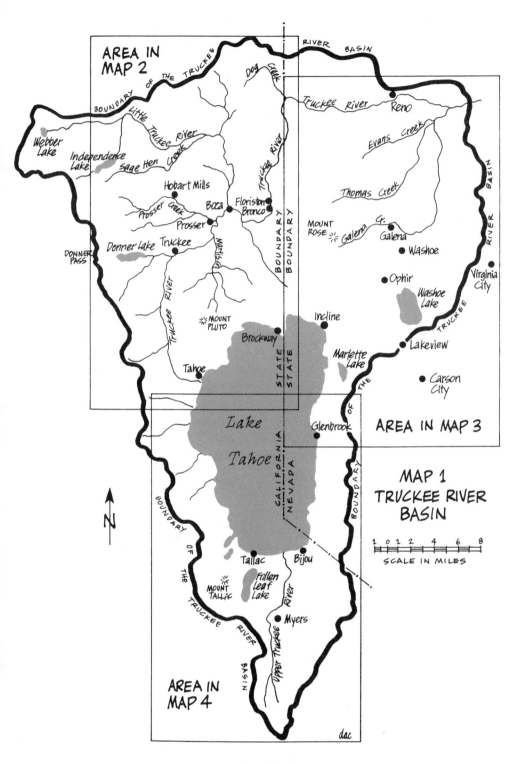

AREA IN
MAP 2

BOUNDARY OF THE TRUCKEE

RIVER BASIN

Dog Creek

Truckee River

Reno

Webber Lake

Little Truckee River

Evans Creek

Independence Lake

Sage Hen Creek

Thomas Creek

Hobart Mills

Prosser Creek

Boca

Floriston

Bronco

Truckee River

BOUNDARY

BOUNDARY

MOUNT ROSE

Galena C.

Galena

Prosser

Donner Lake

Truckee

Washoe

DONNER PASS

Martis

Truckee River

Ophir

Washoe Lake

Virginia City

MOUNT PLUTO

Incline

Brockway

STATE

STATE

Lakeview

Marlette Lake

OF THE

Carson City

Tahoe

AREA IN MAP 3

Lake

CALIFORNIA

NEVADA

Glenbrook

MAP 1
TRUCKEE RIVER
BASIN

Tahoe

1 0 1 2   4   6   8

SCALE IN MILES

BOUNDARY OF

Tallac

Bijou

THE

Fallen Leaf Lake

MOUNT TALLAC

Upper Truckee River

TRUCKEE

Myers

RIVER

BASIN

AREA IN
MAP 4

dac

x

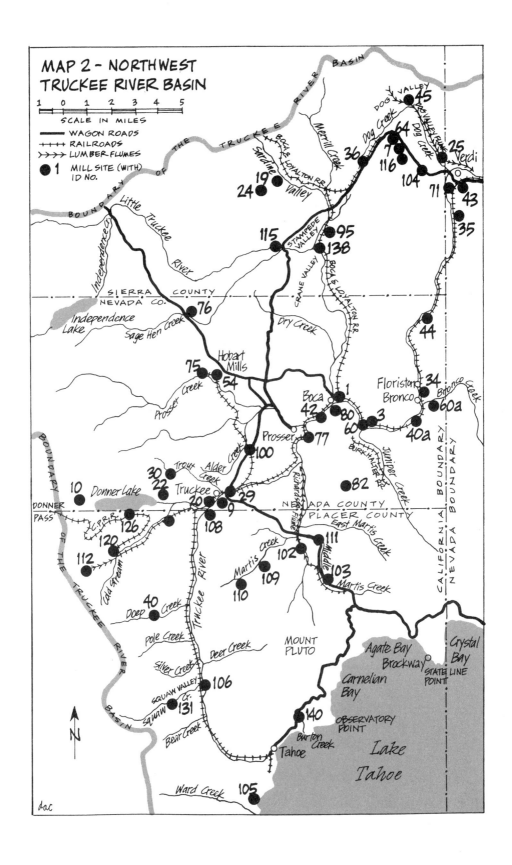

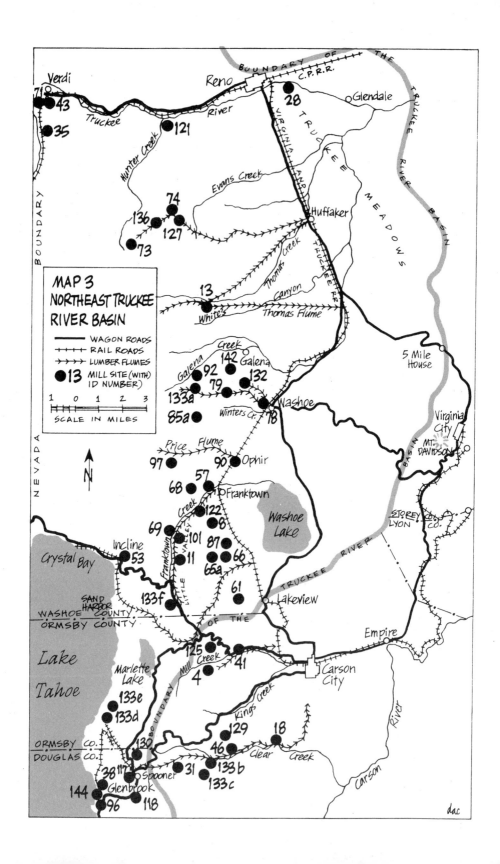

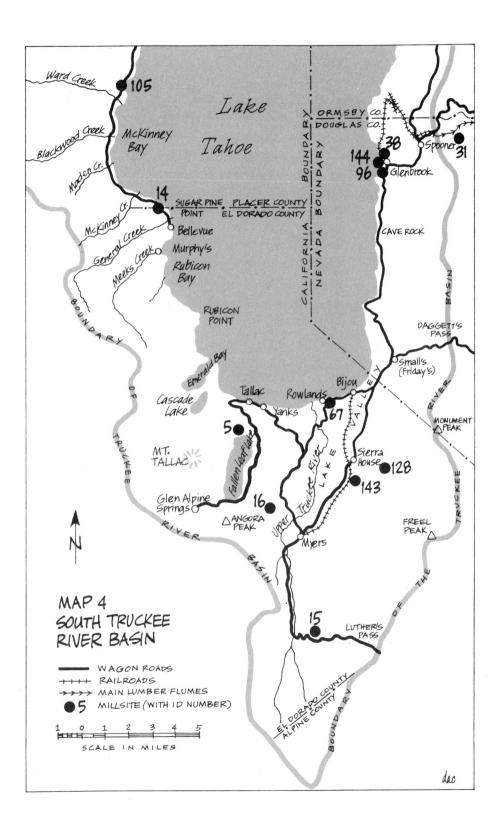

Ward Creek

105

Lake

Tahoe

Blackwood Creek

McKinney
Bay

Madon Cr.

ORMSBY CO.
DOUGLAS CO.

38

144   Spooner   31
96   Glenbrook

McKinney Cr.

14

SUGAR PINE   PLACER COUNTY
POINT   EL DORADO COUNTY

CAVE ROCK

McKinney Cr.

Bellevue

Murphy's

General Creek

Meeks Creek

Rubicon
Bay

DAGGETT'S
PASS

RUBICON
POINT

BOUNDARY

Emerald Bay

Small's
(Friday's)

OF

Cascade
Lake

Tallac

Rowlands   Bijou

Yanks

67

MONUMENT
PEAK

TRUCKEE

5

MT.
TALLAC

Sierra
House

128

16

143

RIVER

Glen Alpine
Springs

ANGORA
PEAK

Upper Truckee River

Myers

FREEL
PEAK

N

BASIN

OF THE TRUCKEE

MAP 4
SOUTH TRUCKEE
RIVER BASIN

15

LUTHER'S
PASS

——— WAGON ROADS
+++++ RAILROADS
→→→→→ MAIN LUMBER FLUMES
● 5   MILLSITE (WITH ID NUMBER)

1   0   1   2   3   4   5

SCALE IN MILES

EL DORADO COUNTY
ALPINE COUNTY

BOUNDARY

dac

1. This sugar pine forest in an adjoining region of the Sierra Nevada is no doubt similar to the prime, virgin stands that once blanketed many acres in the Truckee River Basin. *(Photo courtesy of the U.S. Forest Service.)*

1. Whittling on the Timberlands

*F*or centuries the rustle of wind-tossed foliage and other voices of the wilderness were the dominant sounds in the virgin forests of pine and fir that blanketed the Truckee Basin headwaters. Then, early in the 1850s, forays were made into the eastern border of the forests by settlers from the Washoe and Carson Valleys. Those Nevada farmers rested their plows and took up axes only long enough to hew the timbers and posts needed for buildings and corrals, and to lay in stacks of fuel wood. Those sounds of chopping and of falling trees—intermittent and limited though they were—forecast lasting changes in the forest environment.

Such scattered cuttings were mere nibbles at one edge of the vast timberlands that extended for miles over the Carson Range and on westward toward the crest of the Sierra. More noticeable was the impact of logging after the first several sawmills were constructed where the eastern edge of forest met the sage.

Reputedly the earliest sawmill in the Nevada portion of the basin was built in 1856 by Elder Orson Hyde, leader of the Mormon settlement at Franktown, Nevada.[3] His $10,000 water-powered mill stood half a mile west of the settlement (ID-57). The mill machinery, including two saws—an upright and a circular—was delivered via the pioneer Sierra stage road between Placerville, California and Nevada. After operating it for only a month, during October 1856, the conscientious elder responded to a call to return to Salt Lake City, and rented his mill equipment to Jacob Rose, a Carson River trader. As advance rental fee, Hyde acknowledged receiving "one span of indifferent mules, a worn-out harness, two yokes of oxen and an old wagon," items he required for the trip to Salt Lake City.

In 1862 Hyde attempted to reclaim his mill, then in the posses-

---

3. For documentation of this and other operations, see the Appendix and Sources Cited at back of book.

1

sion of R. D. Sides and valued at $20,000. The attempt at recovery was unsuccessful due to the clouded titles of Mormon property in the Carson area after the creation of the Territory of Nevada.

A contemporary to the Hyde mill was established in 1856 in the California portion of the basin. This was in Lake Valley, El Dorado County, at what became known as Hawthorne Station after the pioneer mill owner, William A. Hawthorne (ID-47). He eventually settled near Walker Lake, Nevada, in a town that now bears his name.

2. Comstock Discovery Triggers Lumbering Boom

*I*n 1859 the exploitation of the Comstock Lode triggered an explosive demand for wood. And within a couple of years an array of sawmills appeared all along the eastern border of the Carson Range. One of these, the first steam-powered sawmill in Nevada, was built by Henry Gregory and James Riddle in the fall of 1859 about 2 miles west of Carson City on Mill Creek (ID-41). (This is the stream now called Ash Creek). The sawmill, reported to have been situated adjacent to a fine stand of timber—doubtless jeffrey pine—was one of those nearest to the Comstock.

An indication of the demand for the output from the Gregory-Riddle mill was a report in the *San Francisco Bulletin* of April 23, 1860: "Were the capacity of the mill four times as great [as 15,000 board feet a day] . . . it could not supply the demand." And if further evidence were needed to demonstrate how the local mining industry hungered for wood—for mine timbers and firewood, as well as for lumber to house its workers—note this comparison made by the *Sacramento Union*: On March 17, 1860 the price of lumber at Virginia City was $100 per thousand board feet; a month later the price had advanced to $300 per thousand.

Two-thirds of the charge for lumber at the Comstock Lode was claimed by teamsters for the haul of some 12 to 18 miles between sawmill and mine. Therefore, some mine owners sought to minimize costs by moving their ore-crushing machinery from the Lode to the timberlands bordering the Washoe Valley. At such installations water from mountain streams was used to power both stamp mills and sawmills. Although in these situations there were high charges for hauling ore west from the mines and across the valley,

2. This view illustrates features of the traditional upright saw. The blade is held taut in a frame that moves up and down in response to power cranked from a steam engine or (as here) from a waterwheel. The saw cuts only on downstrokes, with pauses in sawing at the end of each downstroke while the log is moved forward and positioned against the saw for another cut. This primitive sawmill is not greatly more efficient than a historic, hand-powered whip saw (or pit saw). Probably all upright mills in the Truckee Basin were better equipped than this one, which might deliver only a few hundred board feet a day. *(Photo courtesy of the U.S. Forest Service.)*

3. During the first years of lumbering in the Truckee Basin—in the 1850s and 1860s—mills powered by water shared the total production about equally with mills powered by steam. Daily outputs by each type ranged from several thousand feet to 20,000 feet—even greater. Production depended largely upon the input of manpower and the components of machinery in the mill. The use of a penstock, a turbine or huge waterwheel, for example, might be credited with significant increased output. And even the use of such an item as a windlass (as shown here) might well give a measure of increased production. Most important, certainly,

a circular saw harnessed to a steam engine (as shown here) provided a significant advantage over a linkage of an upright blade to steam. From the beginning of sawing in the basin, circulars that worked continuously on a log were favored by a 2 to 1 margin over uprights that attacked a log in a series of strokes. And by the 1870s most uprights were phased out. Most water-powered mills were also phased out before 1880, and were replaced by steam-powered operations that were not limited by fluctuating streamflow; that also could use mill refuse to fuel boilers. (*Photo courtesy of Nevada Historical Society.*)

part of the hauling costs could be charged to loads of timber and fuel wood that were shipped east on return hauls to the mines located along the barren hills of the Comstock.

An especially ambitious integration of ore processing and saw-milling was by the Ophir Company (ID-90). In April 1861, its mills were established adjacent to two thousand acres of timber west of Washoe Lake. The company employed about a hundred men in forest-based work: cutting and hauling wood, sawmilling, produc-ing charcoal, etc. Many more individuals worked at ore reduction. The company flourished for only a couple of years, however, de-spite a favorable economic climate for both mining and lumbering. Reflecting sometime later on that short-lived venture, the *Mining & Scientific Press* reported in February 24, 1877 that the managers "had . . . outgrown their income."

A much more successful contemporary venture than the Ophir was initiated in 1861 by three lumbermen from Maine—the Bragg brothers and a Gilman Folsom (ID-8). Their Central Mill formed the nucleus of a small settlement a mile south of Franktown aptly named Little Bangor. During a decade of operation this mill was evidently the largest single supplier of wood to the Comstock. In 1870 the partners pulled stakes in the Washoe Valley and established a mill site in the heart of the fabulous Truckee River timber at Clinton (ID-60).

Well into the 1860s the boom in lumbering reflected the tempo of Comstock mining. And both industries competed for manpower not preempted for service in the Civil War. The demands for labor in both mines and woods were strong enough to lure a steady stream of manpower to the Nevada-California locale from other regions. No doubt most of those newcomers were attracted west by the promise of wealth at the Comstock. But many who rushed so eagerly to the mines soon learned that the returns from harvesting timber promised a more stable income than those from digging ore. So they traded their shovels and picks for axes and cant hooks. Other new arrivals in the region barely tested their luck at mining— if indeed they even tried it—before they sought a career in lumber-ing. Some of those were men who crossed not only a continent but an ocean as well to reach the California-Nevada border.

Two men of foreign birth who carved successful careers out of Truckee Basin timber were the Marker brothers, Hans and Peter (ID-74a). They came directly to Nevada from Denmark, and for well over a decade they were leading producers of cordwood. From their Galena Creek operations they harvested 10,000 to 15,000 cords of wood annually for delivery to Virginia City.

At the height of this boom period in the first half of the sixties, at least three dozen sawmills were situated along the west side of the Washoe Valley and in the foothills of the Carson Range. These, cutting to capacity, sawed within a range of 5,000 to 30,000 board feet per day. Some operated day and night—Acey Person, for example, who realized an output of 26,000 feet in a 24-hour period (ID-92). Essentially, those pioneer millmen sawed to a limit dictated as much by available manpower as by hard-to-get machinery.

After the sawlogs were harvested, woodcutters salvaged the logging residues for cordwood. Such leavings were more satisfactory sources of fuel than were the scrubby pinyons and junipers found on the desert hills around Virginia City. Moreover, the most accessible of these low-volume stands were soon denuded by Chinese wood cutters who then turned in desperation to bundling sagebrush for use as fuel.

4. Cordwood was an important part of the harvest of forest. A number of operators made a good living by concentrating on cutting cordwood to meet demands of railroads and ore mills in particular for fuel. To accomplish this task an efficient procedure was to glean cutovers after a timber harvest and convert residues into cordwood. Pack mules proved to be ideal carriers for delivery of this secondary harvest to concentration points on railroad or stream bank.
(Photo courtesy of Searls Historical Library.)

3. The Emerging Development Pattern, and the Men Who Shaped It

B y the 1870s sawmills had been established throughout the timbered parts of the basin and the eventual pattern of lumbering development was emerging, as indicated in Maps 2, 3 and 4 on pages xi–xiii. This schematic of the Truckee Basin headwaters includes the eastern portions of the California counties of Sierra, Nevada, Placer, and El Dorado, and a tiny piece of Alpine County. Western portions of the Nevada counties of Washoe, Douglas, and Ormsby (now Carson City) are also included. Identification numbers indicate locations of most sawmills and related operations that were sited in the Truckee Basin during the last half of the nineteenth century and the early decades of the twentieth.

Lumbering mill sites are listed alphabetically by owner(s), and/or company name, in the appendix which begins on page 65. Although not a complete inventory of operations in the basin as interpreted from old records, the appendix identifies and describes the large majority of operations during the years when the virgin forests of the area were being liquidated.[4]

The mill owners and operators shown in the appendix were key figures in the lumber industry of the Truckee Basin. Their names, found in documents and publications, are part of the historical record—a record that seldom mentions those who comprised the main working force that converted trees to lumber and other pro-

4. Because it was common practice for joint ownerships of mills, the appendix lists more than one name for some mill sites. Description of such a site is confined to one listing—under the first named owner or operator (the name by which the operation was generally known). Since the information in the appendix is based partly on sketchy records, some corrections may be made by those who dig further into history than the author did. These may involve changes in dates of mill operation and in names of owners or operators. Understandably, just as weathering and cultural changes over the years have destroyed physical remains of most old mill sites, references to some sites in publications and official documents have been partly obliterated by aging. Sites for which records of location are vague are identified by an asterisk (*) next to the identification number, to show they are not on the maps. In some instances mill sites are keyed to obsolete place names that couldn't be located by this author. More persistent researchers may well pinpoint such place names. Incidentally, numbered temporary construction camps established by the Central Pacific Railroad have been carried by some maps over the years, and they proved to be useful landmarks for referencing mill sites.

5. A Healthy group of the men who made sawdust at the Glenbrook mills in the 1870s through the 1890s. Their names didn't appear on the letterhead of the Carson and Tahoe Lumber and Flume Company. But the record shows that this crew and co-workers produced far more lumber, mine timbers and ties than any other group of mill workers in the Truckee Basin. And they loaded those stacks of wood products on a narrow-gauge railroad for the first link of the smoothly run marketing system controlled by those outstanding lumbermen: Yerington and Bliss. *(Photo courtesy of Nevada Historical Society.)*

ducts. For the most part, the fallers, the sawyers, the buckers, the teamsters, the river hogs, the grease monkeys, the donkey punchers, the whistle punks, and the pond men are lost to history. The list of workers goes on. Only a few of those—primarily a sample selected by fate as centerpieces in the accidents that plagued the operations of logging and milling—have been recognized by reporters. As examples of these exceptions, from the yellowing pages of old newspapers come the names of two men who earned obituaries the hard way. In June 1867, Hiram Coldwell, a logger at the Wagner-Klein operation (ID-135) was crushed when a log caught him during its drop from wagon to landing. And, in 1898, James Sherrick, an engineer employed by the Larrity-Hall-Revert mill (ID-62), was blown into eternity when a boiler exploded.

The headwaters portion of the Truckee Basin is historically a forest zone where lumbering once dominated the economy. As represented in Map 1 (page x), the eastern boundary of this zone is arbitrary, drawn to include the agriculture and mining developments that rounded out the economy of the headwaters. Also included is the Clear Creek drainage and several small drainages north of Clear Creek, because of close geographic ties to the basin. Within that forest zone is an appreciable acreage of undeveloped open land—mainly alpine barrens near the crest of the Sierra, and sagebrush openings along the northern and southeastern borders.

The sites of sawmills were concentrated within portions of that zone. As shown in Maps 2, 3, and 4 (pages xi–xiii), the pattern of mill sites was for good reasons oriented primarily along main streams. Such a pattern insured easy access to water to power machinery, to supply boilers, to float logs or lumber, as well as for domestic use. No doubt the concentrations of mill sites suggest where the best timberlands were situated, since the lumbermen aimed to keep length of log hauls to a minimum.

6. The destiny of every lumber camp was controlled by the mix that came out of the kitchen. If the crew in white jackets delivered just two meals in succession that were less than huge or of questionable aroma, the timekeeper could promptly be facing a lineup of the other crews demanding their severance pay.
(Photo courtesy of Searls Historical Library.)

4. Lumbering Prospers as Mining Slumps

*I*n the latter 1860s, when Comstock mining activities declined due to depletion of easily-mined ore bodies and water-flooded tunnels, the demand for mine timbers naturally dropped. Consequently, some lumbermen closed operations in Nevada and moved to other areas. Several leading operators chose the Truckee vicinity, anticipating the long-term boost that the building of the Central Pacific Railroad would give to lumbering in the heart of the basin.

Despite the slump in Comstock activities, there was still a strong demand for wood. Aside from continuing substantial requirements of mining interests, there were active markets for lumber and fuel wood at settlements in the Carson and Washoe Valleys. Consequently, some Nevada lumbermen actually expanded operations. Captain A. W. Pray was one of them. With C. R. Barrett and N. D. Winters as partners, he had built a plant at Glenbrook on the Nevada shore of Lake Tahoe in 1861 (ID-96). This mill was known as the Lake Bigler Lumber Company.[5] In 1862 Pray bought out the interests of his partners and increased his timber holdings by purchasing three large tracts belonging to the original locators of Glenbrook: Warren, Murdock, and Walton. Pray's mill could turn out 20,000 feet per day. Its two circular saws, edger and lathing machinery were driven by water power until 1864, when a conversion to steam was made.

5. Animal Logging in the 1860S, Variety in the Mills

*L*ogging techniques at Pray's operation were similar to those of his contemporaries. Teams of horses or oxen were used to skid logs from stump to mill, except for logging a tract across the lake from his mill. There, logs skidded to the lakeshore were rafted and towed to the mill by steamer. Transport of sawn products from Pray's mill to market was by teams and wagons over the Kings Canyon toll road that terminated at Carson City.

5. Lake Bigler was the official name for Tahoe from 1854 until 1945, when the California legislature finally adopted the name which has been in popular use ever since 1862.

7. From the days when logging began in the basin until late in the nineteenth century, animals provided most of the power for yarding. And for direct skidding oxen were usually preferred. Frequently bulls were also preferred for pulling loads of logs by wagon (as here). By this method a bull team could easily move several times the weight of logs it could move by skidding. The option of using wagons was limited to gentle terrain. Within that constraint, log hauls by wagon have been used right up to the present, long after animals were replaced by other power sources. *(Photo courtesy of Nevada Historical Society.)*

Reports of lumbering in the 1860s indicated that the number of mills powered by water was about the same as those driven by steam. From the 1870s onward, there was a gradual shift to steam. Obviously, water was used most effectively where streamflow was relatively constant. This was the situation, for example, on Galena Creek, where in 1862 the firm of Stiltz, Ramsey and Company ran both a sawmill and stamp mill on power from a single waterwheel 50 feet in diameter (ID-2). Also in the 1860s, Augustus Saxton and his son Reuben made effective use of an overshot waterwheel 54 feet in diameter at their mill site on the western shore of Lake Tahoe (ID-105). By the 1870s, the Saxtons had converted to steam power. Such conversions by no means indicated that water-powered mills

8. The McGiffert Loader is shown here loading logs onto a string of flats. This machine and several similar machines have greatly simplified and speeded up the job of log handling over the historic technique of parbuckling: the procedure whereby a log is rolled up an incline to the bed of a carrier through pressure on a pair of ropes or belts. Through the years a simple procedure for unloading logs has been to remove any ties of logs to the carrier, then dump the load by tilting the carrier sideways. *(Photo courtesy of Nevada Historical Society.)*

9. This Gin Pole Loader performs the job of log handling essentially as does the McGiffert, though the rigging is different.
(Photo courtesy of Searls Historical Library.)

were obsolete by the 1870s. Indeed, during that decade they were still being erected. One notably successful mill was constructed in 1872 by Martin and Hall on Prosser Creek for use by two prominent lumbermen, Oliver Lonkey and E. R. Smith (ID-75). This mill was powered by a water-driven turbine.

Both circulars and upright blades were in general use as head-saws. In both types, a power-driven carriage forced the log against the saw. No mills were operating with such techniques as hand power, windlasses or suspended weights to move the log. Indeed, very few Truckee Basin operators ever used such primitive methods. Nevertheless, techniques were decades away from such efficient machinery as steam-driven carriages, teamed with fast-running band saws, to whisk boards off a log.

Other significant improvements were on the horizon in both logging and marketing, and by the mid-1860s they were being realized.

6. Rivers of Wood

*F*or almost a decade, although the lumber industry was healthy, it was evident that a couple of bottlenecks were holding back production and must be overcome: (1) Faster and more reliable methods were needed to carry forest products to market, and (2) Better methods were required to speed up and simplify delivery of logs to the mill.

The bottleneck in delivery of products to market was corrected first. For several years some lumbermen had pursued a promising technique for solving this problem: the use of a flume for transporting wood. They first used a U-shaped flume, but were frustrated by frequent jamming of boards, timbers and cordwood as the current carried them along the square configuration of the flume. Jams occurred especially at angles where the flumes changed directions. After some testing, several lumbermen discovered that a flume that was V-shaped in cross-section solved the jamming problem, since in that configuration the current consistently forced pieces of wood to float freely upward whenever they touched part of the flume.

An excellent description of the V flume and its operation appeared in Eliot Lord's 1883 monograph for the U.S. Geological Survey, entitled *Comstock Mining and Miners:*

> To form this [V] flume rough planks 1½ inches thick, 24 inches in breadth, and 16 feet long, were joined at an angle of 90 degrees, and the trough thus made was lengthened by the junction of similar sections with overlapping ends. [In improved versions the sections were made to abut.] The flume was laid on the ground with simple wooden props, and supported by trestle-work when ravines were crossed. . . . Sawmills were erected at suitable points in the mountains, and the timbers were then borne down to the valleys, like firewood, from the summit of the Sierras. At first the descent of the flume line was only 1½ inches to the rod, and in order to maintain this grade they wound about hills, skirted the edge of precipices, and crossed deep canyons on lofty trestles. Timbers and wood glided down the current, at short intervals, in a long procession, without crowding or jamming against one another, until they were thrown forth at length from the end of the flume upon a dump in the valley. But when reservoirs stored the mountain drainage, and with creek and lakes supplied strong

flowing streams, then the grade of the flumes was raised in places to an elevation of four feet to the rod and the waterfall was a sheet of foam. Massive timbers thirty-two feet long were hurled down these rapids like arrows from a bow, while the flume trembled with their motion and the water was banked up before them in white curling mounds like breaking surf.

J. W. Haines, a lumberman who operated just outside the eastern border of the Truckee Basin, appears to have made the best claim to developing the V flume. However, his application for a patent stirred up enough litigation to demonstrate that a number of men evidently contributed to the development of the structure. No doubt some were lumbermen in other regions. Evidently the following Nevada millmen had hands in this development: J. R. Knox, Oliver Lonkey, Charles Gillis, and J. R. Goff. Although the man who first used the V flume may be in question, it is clear that the technique was promptly adopted as an efficient replacement for the

10. Spooner Station on the divide between Lake Tahoe and the Carson Valley. The locomotive (center) stands at the terminus of the narrow-gauge line originating at Glenbrook. Here lumber and other wood products are unloaded and transferred to the Clear Creek Flume (foreground). The hills in the background were deforested prior to 1880, the date of this photograph. Though prospects for restocking don't appear promising, note possible seed source in scattered trees on skyline. *(Photo from V&TRR Collection, Carson City, NV.)*

11. Same view as previous photo, but about 60 years later, circa 1940. The partially restocked hillsides demonstrate the reforestation possibilities when there is a seed source and fire protection. *(Photo courtesy of U.S. Forest Service.)*

12. Same view as the two previous photos. This view (circa 1985) demonstrates natural restocking, albeit slow, after deforestation about a century earlier.

13. Clear Creek Flume and flume tender's cabin. In this terrain the building of a few small trestles permits straight-line construction. (*Photo courtesy of Nevada Historical Society.*)

costly hauls by lumber wagons over mountain roads that were very difficult to construct and maintain.

Soon a network of flumes spread over the hills. Many structures were erected primarily to gather water—often from minor drainages—and to feed it to major wood-carrying flumes. In many situations the input from several feeder flumes was required to build the head of water necessary to sustain a payload of timbers.

Only a few structures carried as great a volume of water as that in the flume in Clear Creek. That flume was supplied in part by two large feeder flumes: one from Marlette Lake on the north, another from the terrain south of Clear Creek.

The demonstrated success of the V flume helped attract more lumbermen to the Nevada portion of the basin. During the 1860s and on into the 1870s the following establishments were among the most active in Nevada: the Excelsior Mill (Hobart and Marlette) in Little Valley (ID-51); the mill of Haynie and Company (ID-69) and the Dyer mill (ID-26) in the same locality; Price's mill at the foot of Slide Mountain (ID-97); and the Pacific Wood, Lumber, and Flume Company of Mackay and Fair, with a large mill on Hunter Creek (ID-73), and another on Evans Creek (ID-74). These mills all contributed to the rivers of wood that surged through V flumes down to the Washoe Valley, and to the Truckee Meadows south of Reno.

According to Bancroft's *History of Nevada, Colorado, and Wyoming* (1890), the total length of flumes serving the eastern slope of

14. Lumber yard at lower end of Clear Creek Flume on outskirts of Carson City. Transhipments onto the V&TRR went mostly to the Comstock Lode (on skyline). Some went to CPRR in Reno, circa 1880. *(Photo from V&TRR Collection, Carson City, NV.)*

the Carson Range exceeded 80 miles by 1879. And in that year those flumes carried more than 170,000 cords of wood and over 33 million feet of lumber.

One flume built for Mackay and Fair was 15 miles long. It had a daily carrying capacity of 500 cords of wood, or half million feet of lumber from mills in the Carson Range to Huffaker, in the valley south of Reno. This flume of rugged construction was maintained by strategically stationed repair crews that were alerted by telegraph to situations requiring attention. Consequently, the flow of wood in sizes up to 40 feet in length was seldom interrupted.

Once the problem of marketing was resolved on the Nevada side of the basin, the solution was promptly applied on the Cal-

15. Looking toward the upper end of a donkey chute, against the flow of logs. Note branch chute coming in at right. Spool post, on the right, is sunk in the ground and heavily braced. Such posts hold the main line close to the chute on curves to prevent logs from jumping out of the chute. (*Photo courtesy of U.S. Forest Service.*)

ifornia side. Meanwhile, resourceful lumbermen gave serious attention to that other problem: the tedious transport of logs to the mill.

7. Evolution of Log Chutes

L umbermen were satisfied to use oxen or horses to drag logs directly to the mill during the early stages of a logging show. But as they reached further from the mill for trees, across acres of cutover, it became increasingly difficult to provide steady supplies of logs to feed headsaws; this despite such measures as peeling logs in the woods to permit easy skidding. Consequently, to increase efficiency, logs were channeled into regular skidways instead of being dragged indiscriminately across terrain. To speed up

16. Debris littered yarding area where logs were assembled and skidded to the chute. Note bull block post where the donkey engine was anchored, in right center of view.
(Photo courtesy of U.S. Forest Service.)

yarding, skidways were lined with two parallel series of small trees or poles. These were neatly notched together at the ends and were slabbed on the inside faces. To further facilitate passage of logs as teams pulled them along, the skidways were greased with tallow. Thus was the log chute born, a skidway along which teams of horses (sometimes in tandem) could move an end-to-end series of logs. A hook into a rear log in the series, fastened to the traces, provided the link for moving the logs along the chute. It also was the means, when yanked out, of releasing the team from the logs.

Frequently ox teams were used to drag logs short distances from stump to the head of a horse chute. Where topography permitted, horse chutes often served to deliver logs directly to the log deck at the mill. On many logging shows, however, each horse chute delivered logs into a gravity chute. At that point the hook on the last log was pulled free as the series of logs took flight down the gravity chute and into a mill pond or dam. On some chutes the slope was so great that the streaking logs threw off smoke and sparks.

It may be noted that the chute method of yarding caused minimal ground disturbance and was less destructive to the residual stand of trees than was skidding across the terrain more directly from stump to landing or to the mill. An exception to this condition prevailed where converging skid trails gouged the terrain at the head of a chute.

17. Upper end of donkey chute. Note that on this operation the main yarding was by engine. Horses were used only to make up trails of logs. *(Photo courtesy of U.S. Forest Service.)*

18. Typical chute built for horse logging only. Ideally, on such operations any adverse grades must be gentle and short. Note horse path on the right. *(Photo courtesy U.S. Forest Service.)*

19. A trail of logs arriving by horse chute to a landing. Note chain spiked to the last log in the series—the key to hauling and release of the whole series. From the appearance of horse track, evidently the chute has been well used. Doubtless this qualifies as the type of chute illustrated in Photo 18, where adverse grades are gentle and short. Note the trestle supporting a section of chute in right background. *(Photo courtesy of Searls Historical Library.)*

8. Prime Timber, Cheap Stumpage

The widespread adoption of log chutes in the late 1860s was almost coincident with laying of rails for the Central Pacific through the heart of the Truckee Basin. The arrival of the railroad signaled that the time had come for exploitation of some of the finest timber in the West to meet an overwhelming demand for ties, locomotive fuel and housing in the towns that sprang up along the railroad. As reported by the *San Francisco Call* of March 27, 1878, 300 million feet of lumber was required just for construction of the 40 miles of snowsheds that sheltered the tracks of the Central Pacific across the Sierra summit.

During this period, when the railroad's demands for timber began to peak, came news of hardships for unemployed workers at the Comstock; hardships, nonetheless, that favored workers in the timber industry. During the fierce winter of 1866-67, exceptional demands for fuel wood pushed prices to such a peak that shipments from California were sought to supplement the cordwood produced in the Carson Range. And although mining went into a slump for several years beginning in 1867, with a corresponding dampening of the local market for timber, by 1869 Virginia City was clamoring for lumber to replace buildings destroyed by a devastating fire.

Inevitably the news of all these demands for timber attracted a crowd of millmen, loggers, and would-be lumbermen. Moreover, appetites for lumbering were whetted by reports of the choice pines that grew around Tahoe's shores and along the banks of the Truckee: the ponderosa pine, and the jeffrey pine (that sturdy tree with the pleasant, fruity smell to its bark); above all the sugar pine (the fabulous tree with the soft white wood that was so easy to mill and finish). Doubtless, some in this crowd of lumbermen had read the reports by Theodore Judah, the civil engineer who had surveyed the location for the Central Pacific across the Sierra. In enthusiastic terms he wrote that "the sugar pine ... often runs 125 feet high without a limb, and often measures 8 feet through at the base."

Although the jeffrey and sugar and ponderosa pines were favorites, lumbermen soon found that there was a market for some associated species as well. Provided trees were large enough, lodge-pole pines, white firs, and red firs were suitable for square sets in the mines. To qualify for those sets designed by Philip Deidesheimer,

25

dimensions of timbers had to be seven feet in length and sixteen inches on each side.

It wasn't only the reports of fabulous timber supplies coinciding with active demands for forest products that drew loggers to the Truckee area during the decade of the sixties—that was also a time when timberlands could be acquired for nominal prices—even for free.

A major source of cheap timber was the tremendous acreage of land granted to the Central Pacific by the federal government: the alternate sections through a strip 20 miles wide on each side of the rail right-of-way. The going price for such land—including much prime timber—was only $1.25 per acre. Naturally the Central Pacific was eager to dispose of this land to lumbermen, since, aside from returns from the land sales, such transactions encouraged the harvest of forest products needed to satisfy demands of the railroad.

Even more attractive sources of supply for some lumbermen were all lands—both public and private—within the Central Pacific 400-foot-wide right-of-way, centered on the railroad. By government agreement, the Central Pacific was permitted to take, without charge, materials from that zone, provided such materials were used in railroad construction. Thus, lumbermen contracted to convert trees from that zone into ties and other wood products required by the Central Pacific.

Other major sources of cheap timber were from stands growing on preempted and homesteaded lands. Although the law intended that these properties be retained in parcels of no more than 160 acres each (preempts bought for $1.25 per acre, homesteads free except for filing fee), many tracts were quickly sold to lumbermen for consolidation into large holdings. Such transfers of ownership, though technical violations of the law, were generally accepted on this frontier as desirable acts to encourage development and settlement of the region.

Some homesteads, after being logged, were quite suitable for the agriculture intended by the homestead law. Indeed, at lower elevations in the basin a thriving livestock industry was based on pastures converted from cutovers. On the other hand, "homesteads" higher in the mountains were dubious candidates for agriculture, and often the only significant returns from filing on such properties were those derived from lumbering. More about this matter later.

So, in an environment that favored lumbering, the loggers had at it. And whenever they chopped their way into a clearing, or into a stand of trees where other men were swinging axes, they veered away into another stretch of forest—not usually difficult to find. And since trees were so cheap on the stump, who was likely to protest if this expanded cut led to a minor trespass, when each stump pasture demonstrated another success in converting the wilderness into profit?

In the forefront of the lumbermen who began harvesting the choice pine and fir in the heart of the basin were several who moved in from the eastern slope of the Carson Range.

George Shaffer was one of those farsighted men, one who became acquainted with the interior of the basin in 1864 when he contracted to bring the first locomotive—the *San Mateo*—across the Sierra. According to Edwards' *Tourist Guide*, he took it in sections on sleighs over the newly completed wagon road that connected Cisco with Coburn Station (the original name for the town that was renamed Truckee in August of 1867). Shaffer had been operating a sawmill built in 1861 on Clear Creek. In 1867 he moved the machinery to Truckee and, with Joseph Gray, erected the first mill in that vicinity on the south edge of town (ID-108).

Gilman Folsom and Charles Bragg, who had operated at Franktown (ID-8), packed their mill equipment in wagons in the late 1860s and moved to Clinton, west of the state line, where they were soon two of the leaders in the industry (ID-60). Oliver Lonkey was another who moved, accompanied by a band of French-Canadian woodsmen. He went from Ophir in Nevada (ID-68,69) to the Verdi-Dog Valley area of California, where he became a leading, highly respected lumberman (ID-70,71,75,76).

There were others who seized opportunities for harvesting timber along the Truckee River. Some of these had backgrounds in lumbering on the west side of the Sierra, notably the Towle brothers, who built the first sawmill at Dutch Flat in 1858, and relocated at Donner Lake in 1867 (ID-126). Another westside lumberman was E. J. Brickell, who, with W. H. Kruger for a partner, had been operating a sawmill at Dutch Flat. Brickell, a restless, active personality, had engaged in a variety of work since arriving in California in 1850. He'd been a hotel keeper, a packtrain operator, a merchant—on balance with only limited success in any endeavor. Finally he found in sawmilling something to capture his interest and effectively

20. W. H. Kruger, who with partner E. J. Brickell guided the Truckee Lumber Company for many prosperous years of operation. *(Photo courtesy of W. H. K. Dunbar, Rio Vista, CA.)*

21. The department store that a lumberjack headed for to get whatever he figured might be found on a shelf—be that crackers or saddle blanket. This particular establishment belonged to W. H. Kruger before he concentrated his business skills as co-manager of the Truckee Lumber Company. *(Photo courtesy of W. H. K. Dunbar, Rio Vista, CA.)*

channel his energies. With what was to prove sound judgment, he foresaw a rewarding destiny if he were to move to the Truckee Basin. After failing to persuade his partner Kruger to join him in a move at that time, he went to Truckee in the fall of 1867 and promptly purchased an interest in the sawmill of George Geisendorfer (ID-9). Success was inevitable. These partners concentrated immediately on contracts for the Central Pacific, in 1868 producing 10,000 ties and two million feet of bridge timbers. Their firm, known as the Truckee Lumber Company, also cut eight million feet of lumber in that year—a healthy share of the total of 66 million feet produced by the dozen companies located in the immediate vicinity of Truckee.

9. The Booming Seventies and Eighties

*F*or twenty years the lumber industry in the Truckee Basin had been maturing, and it came of age in the 1870s. Mills were active in every major tributary of the Truckee River and in many minor drainages as well. In drainages where there were no mills, likely as not there were skidroads leading to sawmills sited not far beyond nearby ridges. And if axes were not reducing trees to logs in those drainages, in all probability they were carving out other forest products: fuel wood, shingle bolts, or charcoal billets.

From the 1880s onward, almost all mills were powered by steam. A primary reason for abandoning water as a power source was to incorporate a procedure feeding upon mill residues, a procedure not limited by fluctuations in stream flow.

Pricing for timberlands in the 1870s and 1880s increased from the $1.25 per acre that was common in the 1860s. Nevertheless, considering the strong demand for wood products, stumpage was still available at bargain rates. Sales of prime timberland situated on terrain favorable for logging were generally well below $10 per acre. Note, as examples, the purchases by several leading lumbermen. In 1875 Oliver Lonkey bought a section of Central Pacific Railroad land for only $5 an acre, and in 1876 George Shaffer paid $7 an acre for a section of railroad land. In the early 1880s the Richardson brothers purchased several sections for prices ranging from $4 to $8 an acre. And as late as 1888 McKay and Stewart acquired half a section of railroad timber for only $4.50 an acre. Even as late as 1893 Lonkey added to his extensive holdings with a purchase at only $20 per acre. All these buys were for parcels of some of the finest timberlands in the West.

Despite brief slowdowns in mining, lumbermen continued to enjoy good markets at the mines. Thanks to the Big Bonanza of 1873, a declining demand for timber at the Comstock was reversed. And in the 1880s, after the richest ore bodies had been depleted, mining of low-grade ores brought a resurgence of trade in square sets and fuel wood at Virginia City.

At the same time there was a continuing demand for replacement of mine timbers that decayed very rapidly under the high heat and humidity persisting in such hardrock mines as the Comstock. Replacements in such circumstances have proven to be necessary at intervals of only several years. Indeed, under some severe conditions, decay reduces such intervals to only a few months.[6] Naturally replacements of timbers become necessary even where mines are operated only intermittently.

A development that greatly reduced costs of wood deliveries to the Comstock was the completion in 1870 of the railroad between Carson City and Virginia City. As reported by the *Gold Hill Daily News* on January 8, 1870, the price of wood delivered to Virginia City fell immediately from $15 to $11.50 per cord. Shipments to the mines were further reduced in cost in 1872 when broad-gauge rail service was inaugurated between Reno and Carson City over an extension of the Virginia and Truckee line.

During the 1870s and 1880s leading lumber companies made significant deliveries to markets well beyond the Truckee Basin. This trend followed closely upon ventures into secondary manufacturing by several firms, especially by those sited adjacent to the river and railroad in the heart of the basin. These operators included the Pacific Wood and Lumber Company (Bragg and Folsom), the Boca Mill Company, Lonkey's Verdi Lumber Company, Shaffer, Richardson Brothers, and Elle Ellen.

The Truckee Lumber Company was a pacesetter from a turning point in 1873. In that year Geisendorfer sold out his share of the company he founded, and Brickell persuaded William Kruger, his former associate, to leave Dutch Flat and buy into the firm. Kruger, an emigrant as a youth from Germany, was endowed with good shares of initiative and intelligence. He had been prospering at the

---

6. Ted Clutter, "Hardrock Timber," *American Forests*, August 1986.

22. Alder Creek Mill. A typical establishment during the heyday of
Truckee Basin lumbering. The capacity of such a mill would generally
be in the range of 20,000 to 40,000 feet per day. The life of the operation
was determined mainly by access to timber supplies. That, in turn,
might well depend upon the number of other nearby operators in
position to exploit those supplies. Take the Alder Creek drainage, for
example. At least three companies were operating here in 1901.
Evidently two mills, Hobart and Davies, had just begun operating at
that time. A third mill (Elle Ellen's) ceased cutting here in that year.
The records are not clear on when the other two mills ceased cutting,
but it might be assumed that they cut out early in the 1900 decade.
This assumption rests on another: that most of the timber in Alder
Creek had been liquidated before they arrived on the scene. This was
because Ellen's mill sawed from 1883 to 1901; and Roberson and
Machomick, who owned that mill prior to 1883, sawed for 10 years
before that. *(Photo courtesy of Searls Historical Library.)*

31

23. At the turn of the century this Verdi Lumber Company mill operated with state-of-the-art machinery. That inclined conveyor from pond to mill fed logs to one of the few band saws to operate in the Truckee Basin. Adjacent facilities of this thriving lumbering community included a planing mill, a box factory, an engine house, dormitories, a hotel and saloons. All this expansion of the town of Verdi may logically be credited to a French-Canadian, Oliver Lonkey. As a young man, he came to Ophir, Nevada and build a sawmill. That was the first in a series of five that he operated. Lonkey may not have qualified as the dean of Truckee lumbermen—there were others who harvested more trees. But he might well have been the most durable, with more than four decades of continuous lumbering to his credit when he went to his grave in 1905. (*Photo courtesy of Nevada Historical Society.*)

24. Hobart Mills of the Sierra Nevada Wood and Lumber Company had the most comprehensive facilities of any lumbering enterprise in the basin. These included, as shown here, a box factory and kiln. *(Photo courtesy of Searls Historical Library.)*

western—Dutch Flat—terminus of the toll road that antedated the Central Pacific on a route across the Sierra. He had interests in mining and merchandising as well as in sawmilling. But he saw a brighter future at Truckee for an astute businessman. Inevitably, under the joint guidance of the two partners, the Truckee Lumber Company was destined to prosper for more than three decades.

Brickell, a venturesome and resourceful native of Illinois, sparked the logging and milling phases of the operation. Kruger, the well-educated emigrant from Germany and a reserved family man, applied his analytical talents to financial management and markets. Both men were congenial, liked by associates and employees (125 in number during the company's peak production in the 1870s). After the installation of four headsaws, the Truckee mill turned out 50 thousand feet of lumber in a 12-hour day. And by the early 1880s, while still making large shipments of lumber, the company was manufacturing furniture, sash and doors, and boxes—products shipped to such varied markets as southern California, Utah, Texas,

25. Hotel at Hobart Mills. *(Photo courtesy of Searls Historical Library.)*

26. Stage depot, Hobart Mills. *(Photo courtesy of Searls Historical Library.)*

and Central America. Quite possibly, as credited by local news reports, the company at that time had the largest facilities for secondary manufacture of forest products on the Pacific Coast.

The expansion beyond sawmilling into such factories as planing mills, box factories, and sash and door establishments meant that whole communities grew up where the larger mills were sited— communities that were virtually self-sufficient. There were extensive quarters for workers, company stores, repair shops, etc.

In the 1870s a number of shingle mills were established. Some were associated with sawmills, but most were aimed at production of a single product, like Ward and Fletcher's Crystal Peak Shingle Factory, that produced 12,000-15,000 shingles in a day. These establishments brought better utilization to the woods. Mass production of shingles from large portions of a tree were substituted for the products which formerly had been creamed by shake makers from only choice sections of a trunk. Nevertheless, the wasteful procedure of shake production continued well into the eighties and beyond. As the *Mining and Scientific Press* complained on June 27, 1885, shake makers were still wasting great portions of tree trunks— even leaving in the forest whole felled trees that didn't prove to have the straight-grained trunks that favored easy splitting. More significant even than waste of wood in felled trees was the degrading of the forest, thus discouraging further lumbering, since trees felled for shakes were invariably among the best in the stand. Another adverse effect of shake making was the concentration of logging residues that contributed to fire hazards.

27. Manager's house, Hobart Mills.
(Photo courtesy of Searls Historical Library.)

10. Variations in Logging

Maturing of the lumber industry was accompanied by some standardization of techniques. In the 1880s, for example, crosscut saws came into general use for felling and bucking. Axes were still being used for undercuts and limbing. This represented a pattern of operation being adopted nationwide, a pattern that would not be significantly altered until twentieth century loggers were armed with that dream tool for making sawdust—the chainsaw.[7]

Typical harvest-to-market procedures included skidding to the head of a chute by oxen; delivery of logs by horse chute and/or gravity chute to a narrow-gauge railroad or stream; thence transport by rail haul or river drive to the mill. Delivery of lumber and other milled products to mainline railroad was usually over rail spur, sometimes by flume.

With minor modifications, the foregoing procedures were used by the Truckee Lumber Company in harvesting a large timber tract that was located on plateaus above the Truckee River several miles south of town. Logs were snaked by oxen from stumps to horse chutes, thence transported to the edge of the river bluff. There the logs were projected over gravity chutes—often airborne for half a mile before plunging into the river. Then downstream went the logs for several miles to a reservoir, being carried by surges of water released daily from a splash dam operated by the Donner Boom and Lumber Company. The logs were impounded in the reservoir just upriver from the mill until a pond man herded them with pike pole to the log deck. The mill output went by short spur to the mainline Central Pacific enroute to market. Before logging was completed on that tract, the company modified the method for transport of logs to the gravity chutes. In this modification, horse-drawn cars were used to carry logs as far as two miles over a railroad track to the river bluff.

Typical river drives were limited to several miles at most. A major exception was a drive by the Richard Lent Company in the 1870s, where logs were dumped into the Truckee River at a point about six miles below Lake Tahoe. The drive carried for some 25

7. Richard G. Lillard, *The Great Forest*. New York: Alfred Knopf, 1947.

28. River driving was expensive in the Truckee Basin where logs came large and streams ran shallow. Even though drives were timed insofar as possible to coincide with high water, considerable work was often required to deepen channels. Even then, drivers might spend most of their time on the stream fighting off log jams. This crew of jammers was employed by the Boca Mill and Ice Company on the Little Truckee. *(Photo courtesy of Searls Historical Library.)*

miles to the Eastman and White sawmill situated just east of Reno (ID-28). Although this drive placed the wood ideally close to markets, a high price was paid for delivery. Fluctuations in flow of water over that long stretch caused many logs to be stranded, thus requiring long hours of work by rivermen. Also, sinkers—generally valuable logs heavy with resin and heartwood—often were abandoned when long-distance driving proved to be very difficult or infeasible.

A common practice of companies employing river driving was to concentrate during the summer on felling and bucking and delivery of logs to the river for storage until the autumn rains arrived. A typical sight during late summer was one reported by the *Gold Hill Daily News* of August 16, 1875: "The bed of . . . [the] Truckee is filled with sawlogs awaiting the first rise of water to carry them to the mills below."

River driving, even on main streams, was difficult at best, even during high water periods. Loggers of the Boca Mill Company could bear witness to the problems encountered during drives on the Little Truckee River. Only by spending thousands of dollars each season to widen and deepen the stream could a channel for movement of logs be maintained.

Sometimes logs were cut in early spring and were skidded to the river to await the main snow melt. Such was the situation reported by the local paper in mid-April of 1874, when the Truckee Lumber Company had stored four million feet of logs on the riverbanks five miles above town, awaiting the spring freshet.

Most companies shut down their log transport operations during the winter. Not so the Crystal Peak Company, at least during one winter. According to the *Reno Gazette* of December 31, 1879, the owners of the company, Patrick Henry and Frederick Katz, were sledding logs over 2 feet of snow in Dog Valley (ID-45). There is no record to indicate whether the partner carrying the namesake of a revolutionary patriot also brought from the East experience in winter logging to use in the West.

On two large holdings of Yerington and Bliss—owners of some of the best timberlands in the region—techniques were adapted to an uncommon situation. The company mills were located at Glenbrook on the eastern shore of Lake Tahoe (ID-144). Yet one large timber holding was situated directly across the lake in the vicinity of Sugar Pine Point, and another situated near the south end of the lake in Lake Valley. In both holdings, a well-known contractor, M. C. Gardner, contracted to produce a total of 60 million feet of logs.

According to the *Truckee Republican* of June 3, 1875, six million feet were to be delivered in 1875, the remainder at a rate of 12 million annually in subsequent years. Gardner made his log deliveries by skidding or hauling with bull teams and horses to short, broad-gauge rail lines for transport to the lakeshore, where log rafts

29. Mill number one of the Carson and Tahoe Lumber and Flume Company at Glenbrook was the hub of the lumbering empire founded by Yerington and Bliss in 1873. For nearly three decades their loggers and contractors tapped the prime stands of timber on the slopes around Lake Tahoe. With bull teams, horses, chutes and short broad-gauge rail, they yarded logs and cordwood to assembly areas for transshipment by narrow gauge or rafting to Glenbrook. For a dozen busy years, two mills operated at Glenbrook with a combined daily capacity of 150,000 feet. And when the number two mill went up in smoke, the crews fed logs to old number one around the clock to maintain an output approaching the number two mill level. That whole output went by narrow gauge for eight miles to Spooner at the crest of the Carson Range on the first leg of a journey to markets. *(Photo courtesy of Nevada Historical Society.)*

were assembled to be towed by steamer across the water to the mills.

Although most lumbermen preferred to handle both milling and logging, the use of a contractor for logging was not unusual. Specifically, for example, in the Lake Valley area there were two other contractors besides Gardner. William W. "Billy" Lapham devoted part-time to logging, though his main interest was in managing Lapham's Hotel and Landing at Lakeside. George Washington Chubbuck spent more time on logging, but was also in the hotel business as a lessee of the Sierra House.

A large part of the cordwood production was by operators who specialized in that business. A. M. Wicks was one of those operators. His production came from a timber ranch of 790 acres near Bronco. Another leading cordwood producer was Abner Weed,[8] operating in the headwaters of Sage Hen Creek. The Donner Boom and Lumber Company also produced cordwood on a large scale. Perhaps the largest fuel wood operation in the basin was by Sisson, Wallace and Company. They employed over 350 Chinese to cut wood and make charcoal near Truckee. In 1874 between 1,000 and 2,000 bushels of this fuel were shipped weekly to Virginia City.

One of the most spectacular techniques in lumber transport was introduced in 1880 by the Sierra Nevada Wood and Lumber Company. This outfit, destined to be the leading lumber producer in the basin, used an endless cableway to carry lumber for 4000 feet from its mill on the north shore of Lake Tahoe to the top of a high ridge in the Carson Range. After going through a tunnel, the lumber was flumed down the eastern slope of the range to Lakeview on the Virginia and Truckee Railroad. The mill site took its name of Incline from the cableway and was a showpiece for its owners, W. S. Hobart and S. H. Marlette. These lumbermen had holdings adjacent to the lake so extensive that, according to the *California Illustrated Times* of December 25, 1877, "The number of acres of forest they own may be computed by the tens of thousands."

An innovation in logging introduced by the Richardson brothers was a steam wagon that ran on flanged wheels over wooden rails. Reputedly, this smoke-belching monster with clanging undercarriage scared many a team as it pulled a flatcar of logs from the logging show to the mill. Though steam wagons on wood rails

8. The city of Weed, California was named for him.

41

30. This mill of the Sierra Nevada Wood and Lumber Company was situated at what is now Incline, not far (eight miles north by lakeshore) from the Glenbrook mills. It was a contemporary of theirs, and its output went over the mountains, as did that from Glenbrook, to the Carson Valley. Those factors, and the fact that the two companies shared control of most of the timberlands on Tahoe's slopes, suggest that these giants were fierce rivals. In fact, the competition was not all that serious, because they concentrated, in the main, on different markets. Most of Glenbrook's production went to the Comstock; most of that from Incline found markets on the route of the Central Pacific, though significant shipments also went to the Comstock. The production at Incline was transported in the first stages by rail and flume, as was the production at Glenbrook. The method of rail transport to mountain top from Incline, however, was straight-line cable-rail; from Glenbrook by switch-back narrow gauge. Note the cable-rail line up the mountain behind the Incline mill. (*Photo courtesy of Nevada Historical Society.*)

served the Richardsons for several years, and were used by a few other operators, they failed to attract most lumbermen, who were more interested in applying conventional railroads to lumbering. Smooth-running rapid transport over steel rails was far more appealing than log rails that were soon reduced to kindling by the drivers.

The Richardsons also developed a method to expedite log handling at the headsaw. Inclined blocks, maneuvered by pulling on a rope, caused the log to be shifted and canted in front of the saw. As reported by the *Mining and Scientific Press* of August 5, 1876, this

31. The Richardson brothers modified a steam wagon to run with flanged wheels on log rails. Since those softwood tracks required frequent replacement, few other lumbermen were interested in the vehicle. Apparently the Richardsons used that vehicle for hauling logs from the logging show to the mill. Another vehicle with regular wheels was evidently used to deliver lumber over an eight-mile haul from mill to box factory and yard in the eastern part of Truckee. In this sketch the artist suggests two roles for the wagon.
(*Illustration courtesy of W. W. Richardson, Reno.*)

technique was patented by the Richardsons and was soon in use by several other lumbermen.

11. Icy Millponds and Cutover Pastures

When the heavy snows arrived at Truckee—usually in November—and the mercury flirted with another record low, most loggers caught the westbound Central Pacific for Sacramento or San Francisco. Some who had it made for the winter looked only for warm and comfortable surroundings in which to wait out the long weeks until the woods dried out again. Others, who had spent their summer wages as fast as they could drag them, hoped for temporary work in the city. However, they were unlikely to fare nearly as well as some loggers who remained in the basin over the winter—those who swapped cork boots for shoepacs and who continued working in familiar surroundings and with familiar tools. From freezeup to breakup they cut ice from ponds where logs had floated in summer. Such reservoirs, after the log debris had been flushed away, were ideal for production of the icy blocks that were shipped both east and west to markets along the railroad. Boca and Verdi were two important ice-producing locations. These mill towns offered large ponds for ice production and good sources of the sawdust required for insulation of ice in transit or in summer storage.

Incidentally, mill ponds served the fishing industry in the Lake Tahoe area. At several locations, ponds created out of portions of lake or stream were used not only to store logs but to raise trout demanded by sportsmen and by suppliers of restaurants in San Francisco and other population centers.

Livestock raising was another lumbering-related activity that flourished in the basin during the last part of the nineteenth century and the beginning of the twentieth. A livestock business quite naturally developed around the lush meadows that hugged many of the stream courses in the basin. And, inevitably, as adjacent forest was harvested, the growth of vegetation in the cutovers provided at least temporary sources of stock feed. Supplemental forage was also derived from natural glades in the timberlands. Many of the livestock enterprises were oriented to dairying, and shipments of dairy products, especially butter, went well beyond the basin.

32. Doan Steam Wagon. This tricycle model was more popular than the Richardson wooden rail model. Here it is shown taking lumber by road from a mill in Dog Valley to the headquarters of the Verdi Mill Company in Verdi. *(Photo courtesy of Nevada Historical Society.)*

33. At Hobart Mills a somewhat different version of steam wagon with trailers was used for lumber transport. (*Photo courtesy of Searls Historical Library.*)

12. Consolidation and Winding Down

For two prosperous decades—during the 1860s and 1870s—settlements followed the pattern dictated by lumbering in the Truckee Basin. Towns mushroomed quickly in virtually every locality where mills began sawing, and by the 1880s the general pattern was set. Then, inevitably, from the 1880s onward, as the mills devoured their birthrights, associated towns withered and died: Boca, Franktown, Galena, Huffaker, Mill City, Ophir—the list goes on of once active towns that now are only place names on a map. A few lumbering centers survived and continued to prosper: Truckee, Verdi, Incline, and Tahoe City—a handful that built a future primarily on tourism.

In the last decades of the nineteenth century, the lumber industry of the basin was dominated by a dozen or so large companies. In large part due to dwindling timber supplies, some well-known companies ceased operation by the 1880s. These included the Pacific Wood, Lumber and Flume Company, owned by two of the Comstock Bonanza Kings, John Mackay and James Fair. It took only five years of logging, milling and fluming during the 1870s for the firm to wipe out extensive timber stands in the Hunter Creek and Evans Creek drainages, and its two sawmills closed in 1880 after all the Mackay and Fair timber holdings were liquidated. The company used more than 50 million feet of this harvest just for square sets to replace the ore removed from five Comstock mines: Consolidated Virginia and California, Hale and Norcross, Gould and Curry, Best and Belcher, and the Utah. This estimate was recorded in Dewey's *The Bonanza Mines of Nevada, 1878*.

During the same five year period about 100,000 cords of wood were consumed each season by ore mills at these mines. Meeting this demand required 120 Chinese employees to handle wood transfers at Huffaker. Altogether, about 800 loggers and sawmill workers were employed during peak operation of the Mackay and Fair lumbering enterprise.

Considerable stumpage was still available in the heart of the basin, and prospective wood shortages were only shadows on the horizon. Nevertheless, those vague warnings spurred organizations with spare capital to make consolidated purchases of timberlands. Two farsighted beneficiaries of such consolidations were H. M.

Yerington and D. L. Bliss. They blocked up enough holdings along both sides of the state line to sustain operation of two large sawmills at Glenbrook for a quarter of a century. Their Carson and Tahoe Lumber and Flume Company owned 14 miles of narrow-gauge railroad which carried the mill output to Spooner's Summit. There it was transferred to a flume for a 17-mile journey to the Virginia and Truckee Railroad, which carried the wood to the Comstock.

The Virginia and Truckee Railroad and Yerington and Bliss were closely joined financially through the Bank of California, and Yerington was an executive of the V&T. Thus the lumber company enjoyed preferential rates for rail shipments. This preference obviously worked to the disadvantage of other companies, particularly to small mills located along the Truckee River. Large firms in similar situations were not so adversely affected, most having developed substantial markets outside the Comstock mining complex. Regardless, Yerington and Bliss faced very little competition at the Comstock marketplace after the Mackay and Fair mills shut down.

Notable examples of the individuals and firms that contributed to a competitive industry around the turn of the century were Shaffer, Lonkey and Smith, Elle Ellen, the Boca Mill Company, and Bragg and Folsom's Pacific Wood and Lumber Company. In the early 1900s the Davies mills, with head office at Truckee, were also very active.

Two firms dominated the industry. One was Marlette and Hobart's Sierra Nevada Wood and Lumber Company. Both owners were good businessmen, and lady luck also smiled on them. (Hobart reputedly became a millionaire on the Comstock while still in his twenties.) The company eventually owned 65,000-plus acres of land—an empire within the basin exceeded in size only by the firm of Yerington and Bliss, the other dominant firm, owning about 80,000 acres. Marlette and Hobart marketed a total of a billion feet of timber. Yerington and Bliss cut about three-quarters of a billion, and also half a million cords of wood. Together, these two companies produced nearly one-sixth of the total estimated cut in the basin. No other among the scores of lumbering outfits in the basin even approached the production of those two. To adequately trace the activities of those two titans would require more space than is available within this summary of lumbering within the basin.

In 1894 two leaders in the industry faced the prospect of ex-

34. S. H. Marlette, partner in the firm that bears his name along with that of Walter Hobart, the other co-founder. Marlette for some years held the position of Nevada's surveyor general. As an engineer he participated in a number of water development projects while giving primary attention to his responsibilities as a leading lumberman in the Truckee Basin. *(Photo courtesy of Hobart Leonard, Nevada City.)*

hausting timber supplies adjacent to their main logging operations, although they both had large holdings in more distant locations. Consequently, they arranged a trade. A 5,000 acre tract belonging to the Truckee Lumber Company, lying between Truckee and the Sierra Valley, was exchanged for a similar acreage belonging to the Sierra Nevada Wood and Lumber Company of Hobart and Marlette, lying between Truckee and Lake Tahoe. This swap permitted both companies to continue cutting on land contiguous to their recent cutovers and to use existing transport facilities to supply plants at Truckee and Hobart Mills respectively. According to the January 1894 issue of *Pacific Coast Wood and Iron*, this was one of the largest exchanges of timberlands on the Pacific Coast.

The shutdown of the Yerington and Bliss mills at Glenbrook in the late 1890s marked the death of an industry giant. At the same time, this provided an opportunity for the Truckee Lumber Company to increase its rail facilities. In 1900 the Truckee Lumber Company bought the locomotives, cars, and rails of the Glenbrook narrow-gauge line, shipped them across the water to the lake outlet, then installed them to serve in downriver log hauls to Truckee.

Despite the demise of the huge Yerington and Bliss operations, there were still smaller operators working on timber in the vicinity of Lake Tahoe. H. C. Barton was one such operator. As reported by the *Truckee Republican* on August 26, 1903, he had just moved his 50 lumberjacks and equipment to a logging show in Ward Creek, four miles from Tahoe City. Here, islands of good timber had survived

35. J. B. Overton was a key employee with Hobart and Marlette. He began working for them in the mid-1870s, and was in charge of cutting flume timber for their Excelsior mill. And in 1879 he became superintendent for their new mill at Incline. Later he was general manager at Hobart Mills, a position he held until retirement at the turn of the century. (*Photo courtesy of Hobart Leonard, Nevada City.*)

the cuts by the Saxtons and others who logged in that vicinity as far back as the early 1860s. The Barton operation demonstrated that animal logging was still a viable option, despite increased mechanization in the woods. Barton was reported to be using 64 horses for skidding as the twentieth century began.

13. Steam in the Woods

*A*round the turn of the century a gradual irreversible trend in skidding technique evolved. Less and less often could the sounds of men working with animals be heard on logging operations. The cracking of bullwhips, the shouting and cursing of teamsters, the bellowing of prodded oxen and the snorting of horses were replaced by the growls of yarding engines and the piercing whistles used to signal the donkey puncher that logs were hooked to the mainline. Just as surely as the cutovers were replacing the virgin forest, so were the bull donkeys replacing the bull teams.

Dolbeers, with vertically oriented spools to handle the cable, were the first donkey engines used in the basin. These were employed on several operations, including that of the Verdi Lumber Company in the Dog Valley area, and the Truckee Lumber Company on its last operations in the basin near Donner Lake. Most companies, including the Verdi Company, eventually acquired more modern bull donkeys, thus taking advantage of horizontally oriented spools for more efficient cable yarding than the Dolbeers offered. The popularity of donkey engines and cable yarding was

36. Dolbeer donkey, the first kind of steam engine that replaced horses and bulls in Truckee Basin yarding operations. Note the vertically mounted spool for handling the main line cable. This photo suggests that animals could still be used in cable yarding—for more than hauling water. The role of animals was minor, however, in a fast-running cable show. (*Photo courtesy of Nevada Historical Society.*)

37. Bull donkey, the yarding machine that replaced the Dolbeer. It is more efficient on two counts: (1) the horizontally mounted spool insures even wear on all parts of the spool; (2) the horizontal mounting is sturdier than the vertical mount. Note the larger spool on this bull donkey than on the Dolbeer. *(Photo courtesy of Nevada Historical Society.)*

demonstrated by the operations of Hobart Mills, where by 1917 a dozen Willamette donkeys were in use.

Along with steam-powered yarding came refinements in the layout of chutes. No longer were adverse grades a problem. In fact, uphill grades were preferred to steep downhill grades, where over-running logs might jump the chutes. With steam power on the chute, sharp curves must be avoided where possible, and even on gentle curves, spool posts were required to guide cables.

An unpublished study made in a region adjacent to the Truckee Basin highlights chutes that were similar to those used in the basin.[9] This study describes three types of chutes applicable to donkey logging: the Ridge or Cross-country type, Sidehill type, and Canyon

9. George Raymond Orr, *Logging Chute Study on the Plumas National Forest.* Unpublished ms., U.S. Forest Service, Quincy, CA. 1918.

or Creek bottom type. The first listed, used on relatively gentle terrain, is the least expensive to build and maintain. The other types, as their titles suggest, were generally used in more rugged terrain.

With adequate chute layouts and reasonable operation of power, steam logging resulted in damage to the residual timber stand and to the site that was not seriously greater than damage by animal logging. When skidding was performed without chutes—with logs being dragged indiscriminately across the terrain—damage to the residual stand was naturally greater than with chutes. And some of the steam-powered logging in the basin was of that kind. Inevitably, the cables that systematically and swiftly dragged logs across the terrain did more damage to immature trees than did skidding by animals. Seedlings were ripped out, saplings broken or mangled, thus adding to the denudation contributed by the slash from trees that were harvested. Consequently, on some sites, decades elapsed before second growth was established.

From the early 1900s on, steam engines provided the power for moving logs the whole distance from stump to sawmill. At least that was the procedure on most large operations. This marked an era when railroads came of age in the woods, decades after rail operations on main passenger and trade routes. The full-throated double blasts from highballing locomotives vied with the piercing whistles from bull donkeys to signal the presence of the thriving industry that dominated all activities in the Truckee Basin.

There were a number of the iron horses in use over the years. They came in assorted sizes and shapes. The Climax and Shay and Baldwin were among the most common nameplates. Some were fitted with the 4 feet 8½ inch wide standard-gauge drivers; others with the 3 feet wide narrow-gauge wheels. Still others were bastard gauges. Lumbermen also frequently took advantage of assorted locomotives and cars by installing third rails on roadbeds to provide standard-narrow-gauge combinations.

During the period when donkey engines and trains came into general use, several companies installed band saws (the Verdi Lumber Company and Hobart Mills, among others). Thus, both in woods and mill, lumbering in the basin was accommodating to a nationwide, twentieth-century modernization of the industry.

Yet, paradoxically, the basin's lumbermen were gearing up for an unprecedented rate of harvesting at the very time an end could be seen to the virgin forests that so many had optimistically per-

HOBART LOCOMOTIVES
1902

38. A gathering of train crews and locomotives at Hobart Mills (circa 1900). Obviously, as indicated by slabs in the tenders, these engines were wood burners—as were virtually all that operated during the era of Truckee lumbering. Thus, part of the price lumbermen paid for the convenience of rail transport was the loss of flammable materials near the rails, due to torching by embers escaping from fireboxes. Damages to trestles and to stacks of wood products were not uncommon. (*Photo courtesy of Searls Historical Library.*)

ceived to be virtually limitless. In 1883, Edwards' *Tourist's Guide and Directory of the Truckee Basin* had boasted: "The [timber] supply may be said to be never ending. . . . it is beyond the power of man to estimate when it will be exhausted." By the turn of the century, this viewpoint was being exposed for what it was: overblown optimism.

14. *Fire in the Slash, at the Mills*

*F*ire, of course, has historically been a companion to logging. Thus, as the twentieth century began, it was no new or unusual phenomenon for smoke to lay heavy over the basin all summer, just as it did for many previous summers. And the casual observer might well conclude that fire, not axe and saw, was wiping out the forest. Even when closer observation proved that the whole watershed was not ablaze, the presence of numerous smoke columns pinpointed the locations of many spot fires.

Although lightning caused a number of fires, no doubt most were due to man's activities. Many damaging blazes were escapes from sets for domestic use. Some of the most serious fires fed upon debris in recent cutovers, and owed their origins to sparks from donkey engines or to friction points in cable skidding. Other blazes, feeding on weathered debris in old cutovers, were no doubt also man-caused. Most of the blazes were destined to burn until there was no more fuel to feed upon, or until drowned by the fall rains. Seldom was there any coordinated attempt at fire suppression. Indeed, many of the residents in the basin evidently looked upon wild fires as useful agents in clearing the land of brush and undesirable trees. Moreover, firefighting equipment, when available, was generally inadequate to cope with a major blaze.

Some of the most costly fires occurred along the railroad, where cordwood, ties, mine timbers, or lumber awaited shipment. Such destruction of valuable materials came to be accepted as a price lumbermen paid for pursuing their livelihood. Primary causes of these blazes were cinders from wood-fueled locomotives, despite requirements that fireboxes be closed while trains were passing stores of wood products or were traversing typically tinder dry trestles.

In order to supply locomotives with fuel, large stacks of cordwood were concentrated along every railroad, thus creating high fire hazards. It may be emphasized that just to meet the modest needs of locomotives on the Virginia and Truckee Railroad alone required 800 cords of wood per month. And, according to the *California Illustrated Times* of December 25, 1877, "In a single year the purchases of [Central Pacific] railroad wood have amounted to 75,000 cords at a total cost of $300,000." It may also be noted that to feed the firebox of a logging locomotive for a day's run required about four cords of wood. And by far most of the log hauls by rail in the Truckee Basin were by wood burners. Oil burners were introduced on a few roads—including those of the Hobart Estate—only when lumbering in the basin was drawing to a close.

Very destructive fires also occurred at mills, where burning sawdust and slab piles were constant flammable hazards. Even at the Truckee Lumber Company factories, where good equipment was available for suppressing fires, not only on company property but anywhere in the town, the day came—in 1902—when those factories burned to the ground. Another leading company was even less fortunate. The Pacific Wood and Lumber Company, at what is now Hirschdale, suffered fires two years in succession—first in 1888, when their mill was destroyed and rebuilt, then in 1889, when it was leveled again by fire.

In view of the fire hazards, and the prevalent viewpoints toward burning, it is not surprising that blazes in cutovers ran virtually unchecked through slash and second growth. Consequently, regeneration of forest was delayed for years due to damage to reproduction, both by fire and logging. Fortunately, on many cutovers older trees that were spared during logging provided an abundant seed source. Mostly, these were trees judged to be too defective for utilization. Regardless, degrading of the forest often occurred after logging, as reported by a member of the U.S. Bureau of Forestry who visited the basin in 1904: "The forest is much reduced in density; brush and reproduction are competing for possession of the openings. The sugar pine has disappeared almost entirely.... The finest of the Jeffrey pine and yellow pine and white fir has been removed."[10] Thus, although regeneration of the forest might be anticipated, there was a significant decrease in quality of that forest when compared with the virgin original.

10. E. A. Sterling, *Report on the Forest Condition in the Lake Tahoe Region, California.* June 1904. University of California Forestry Library, Berkeley.

39. Sawmill operators were pleased when the Floriston Pulp and Paper Company began operations in 1900. That mill offered a market for white and red fir. Those were species not favored for lumber, yet they occupied significant areas in some timber stands. Here is the wood yard at Floriston. There's no doubt what species are represented by those four-foot bolts of wood. (*Photo courtesy of Searls Historical Library.*)

15. Pulping the Fir

A significant development in 1900 was the construction of a large paper mill at Floriston (ID-34), financed mainly by the Fleischacker brothers. This Floriston Pulp and Paper Company operated for some 30 years, mainly on white and red fir, species formerly ignored by lumbermen while they concentrated on harvesting pines—the preferred lumber species.

Until 1914, company lands in the vicinity of Duffy Camp provided the main source of wood for the Floriston mill. Operations there, unusual for the Sierra, involved falling and bucking of trees during the early winter. Although this cutting above the snow left many cords wasted in high stumps, there was an advantage in the technique. The harvest was well seasoned by summer, when the wood was carried by pack mules or by wagons to the mill.

Logging was also done in winter, when operations were relocated in an area near Donner Lake after the timber around Duffy Camp was logged off. At the new location the company—now known as Crown-Willamette—used a tramway of buckets (each carrying half a cord of wood) to transport the harvest to the Central Pacific for shipment to Floriston.

Much of the pulpwood used at Floriston was contracted from lumbermen who were pleased to find a market for the fir they might otherwise ignore in logging. Hobart Mills was a major contractor. So was David Smith (ID-112), who had extensive holdings on Coldstream. In 1902 he secured the "largest wood contract ever let in the Truckee Basin," for delivery to Floriston of 50,000 cords of four-foot wood.

16. Axing the Virgin Remnants

F or well over a decade, the symptoms had been evident to those few lumbermen who bothered to study prospects beyond their log decks. And now, as the 1920s appeared on the horizon, there were clear symptoms of a dying industry—an industry that was starving as the loggers stomped into the last prime acres of Truckee Basin timberlands. At the heart of the basin the dust had settled long ago over the skidroads, and dairy cattle grazed side by side with deer on quiet, cutover hillsides. Gone were the shouts of the teamsters and the lowing of oxen. Gone also the sound of logs squealing and smoking down well-greased skidways. Gone also the urgent signals from whistle punks to donkey punchers, the roars of yarding engines and the warning moans of laboring locomotives.

In only a few restricted timberlands were loggers still going at it, slicing away the remnants of the Truckee Basin's virgin stands. Most of the men who reaped a rich harvest during lumbering heydays had departed, seeking other timber bonanzas, or opting for other modes of life. Some also had retired, no doubt comfortably enough if they'd exercised even average business sense. A few, not necessarily liking the prospect, had turned to cutting second growth for a livelihood.

By the 1920s, Hobart Mills was the only company with substantial holdings of timber, enough to insure continuity of operation for more than a decade. All significant competitors—notably Truckee Lumber Company, Verdi Lumber Company, and the Boca Mill—cut out early in the 1900s. During the period from 1900 until it ceased operating in 1936, Hobart Mills maintained an average annual cut of some 25 million feet. Over 90 percent came from the 65,000 acres of company lands, the remainder from timber sales by the Tahoe National Forest. During that period the company continued to modernize equipment both in woods and mill. This included the introduction of tractor logging in the 1930s. That move placed Hobart Mills among the first in the eastern Sierra to adopt that skidding technique.

One lumberman fortunate enough to acquire a piece of virgin timber as late as 1917 was R. G. Gracey (ID-40). He paid the railroad only $45 an acre—for only 40 acres, however. And he may have felt that he'd acquired a bargain as good for his time as were the timber tracts in the basin that went for less than $10 an acre four decades earlier. No doubt, as a grown-on-the-Truckee lumberman, he must have felt just a trace of envy, though, if he tried to equate his parcel of fir on Deep Creek with the prime stands of pine that his forerunners—Shaffer and the Richardsons, for instance—got for their dollars.

Among the handful of other small companies operating during the first decades of the twentieth century were Celio and Sons near Meyers Station (ID-15, 16), Boni and Jackman about 4 miles from Verdi (ID-7), and Watson's Mill near the mouth of Burton Creek (ID-140). The latter cut mainly second growth. None of these opera-

40. Weathered stumps of trees logged in the 1870s were still standing when this photo was taken in the 1930s. They document the slow rate of decay in the desert climate of the Carson Range. They also bear witness to the waste of wood below the snow line, when trees were felled in winter—trees that took over a century to mature. *(Photo courtesy of U.S. Forest Service.)*

tions cut more than half a million feet annually, and most operated for only several years.

When, in November 1936, Hobart Mills whistled farewell to the last log that went through the headsaw, for all practical purposes it signaled the demise of the virgin forest that once blanketed the Truckee Basin headwaters.

Today, vigorous stands of second growth pine and fir, attractions that help lure hosts of visitors to the basin, bear witness to the timber-growing potential of the region. These stands also mark the general areas where virgin forest was cut, and where enough seed trees remained after logging to insure reproduction of the forest; also where that reproduction escaped fires. There are other areas— clear cut, by and large—that are now treeless, and in that semi-desert environment, would seem to have been sage-covered

61

41. In the 1870s and 1880s loggers axed their way above the 8500-foot level on Mount Rose for the meager harvests that might be carved out of subalpine stands. This stump pasture, devoid of reproduction except for herbs and such brush species as sage, ceanothus, and manzanita, may never again yield a crop of timber.
(Photo courtesy of U.S. Forest Service.)

hillsides for centuries. On the eastern slope of the Carson Range, for example, there are such areas.[11] And, hardly believably, not more than half a century ago they were occupied by colonies of stumps bleaching in the sage, mute witnesses to the death of a timber stand some half century before that.

Even an astute observer may find scant evidence on the present landscape of the hectic years when the woods echoed to the thunder of falling old growth trees, to the rumble of logs hurtling down gravity chutes, to the shouts of bullwhackers and to the screams of headsaws slicing logs into boards and ties and mine timbers. Nevertheless, a search along some timbered canyon may reveal

11. R. C. Wilson. *Vegetation Types and Forest Conditions of Douglas, Ormsby and Southwestern Washoe Counties, Nevada.* Berkeley: California Forest and Range Experiment Station, USFS, 1941.

42. William W. "Bill" Bliss stands beside a relic of the mills at Glenbrook, where his great-grandfather, Duane L. Bliss, and H. M. Yerington established the Carson and Tahoe Lumber and Flume Company in the 1870s. These slabs of rock foundation are the only remains of two large mills at this site. Their combined capacity was 150,000 board feet per day.

43. Today, except for this abandoned mill pond, there are no landmarks or artifacts to indicate that this site on the outskirts of Verdi was once a hub of lumbering activity. *(See photo 23 on page 32.)* That bench just beyond the pond was the mill site. When the mill burned to the ground in 1926 it was never rebuilt.

overgrown, converging skidroads, a weathered pile of sawdust, a rusty boiler, or some other fragment of machinery marking the grave of a bygone sawmill. And a scan of some faded newspaper may provide the name of the lumberman who left such a relic after his headsaw delivered the last slice of the last log of the last tree of a remnant of virgin forest in the Truckee Basin.

44. As boss of the highballing logging show of the Sierra Nevada Wood and Lumber Company, George D. Oliver qualified as a big-time Truckee lumberman. That was at the turn of the century when Overton retired and Charles T. Bliss took over as general manager of that prestigious company. Then, in 1914, when Bliss left to manage Tahoe Tavern, Oliver stepped up as manager of the largest lumbering operation in the basin. He continued in that position through a reorganization in 1917 that resulted in a change of name for the firm to Hobart Estate Company. Then, at the close of the logging season in November 1936, when all but slivers of the Truckee's virgin forests had been converted to cutovers, Oliver shut down the operation that Hobart and Marlette began some 60 years earlier. (*Photo courtesy of Searls Historical Library.*)

Appendix A: Lumbering Operations in the Truckee Basin 1856-1936

*L*isted alphabetically by operators or mill names. Identification numbers refer to locations on Maps 2, 3, and 4. Identification numbers followed by an asterisk are not shown on the maps. Sources are listed following the descriptions. See page 84 for full identification of abbreviated source names.

Abbreviations:

CA	California	mi.	mile(s)
CPRR	Central Pacific Railroad	N.	North
cr.	creek	NV	Nevada
dia.	diameter	Op.	Operating dates
E.	East	p(pp)	page (pages)
ft.	board foot (feet)	RR	Railroad
hq.	headquarters	S.	South
in.	inch(es)	Sec(s).	Section(s)
incl.	including	SF	San Francisco
jct.	junction	V&TRR	Virginia City & Truckee Railroad
loco(s)	locomotive(s)	W.	West

1. **AKIN, James, and Latimer E. Doan and D. D. Whitbeck**. Boca Mill & Ice Co. At Boca. Op. 1866–1908. Nevada County holdings incl. W½ of NE¼ & E½ of NW¼ Sec. 28, and W½ of NW¼ of Sec. 4 in T18N R17E. Total holdings along Little Truckee River exceeded 16,000 acres. Logs chuted to river and floated to mill. Employed 30 men to cut and bank timber in winter. Total of 150 employees in summer in woods and mill. Cut in 1879 of 7 million ft., largest reported by mills in California part of Truckee Basin. (Knowles; Edwards; Nevada; MSP; JRP p109.)

   ALDER CREEK Mill. *See A. Proctor* (100).

2* **ALFORD, Wm. and Rusel**. Ramsey Mill. Close to, probably west of, village of Galena, NV. 300 ft. above Stockman's mill and close to Chapin's mill on Galena Creek (also called Mill Creek). Op. 1861–1864? Operated in turn by several lumbermen besides the Alfords; incl. A. H. Wilson, Ramsey, Geo. Stiltz, A. Hattery, Asa Person. Powered by waterwheel 50 ft. in diameter that drove a saw and 20 stamps; later converted to steam. Sawed 20,000 ft. of lumber and crushed 18 tons of rock daily. (MSP 1-11-1862; Kelly 63; Washoe.)

   ALLEN, W. *See Jones & Denton* (59).

3. **ARNOLD, D**. Marysville Mill. 3½ mi. below Boca on Truckee River at Camp 19. Sold to J. R. Rideout in 1868. He sold ⅓ interest to N. Rideout in 1869. (TR 10-3-1868; Nevada.)

4. **ASHE, Alexander**. On Mill Creek (now Ash Creek), NV, near Gregory &

Riddle mill. In SW¼ Sec. 10, T15N R19E. Op. 1860–1871. Waterpowered. Daily cut 20,000 ft. Flooded away and rebuilt in 1861. Occupied by Yerington in 1871–73. (Angel p541; PCBD 1871; GLO T15N R19E, 1865.)

BACHELDER, J. H. *See Burkhart, Bachelder & Gracey* (12).

5. **BALDWIN, Elias Jackson "Lucky."** At NW end of Fallen Leaf Lake. Op. 1880s. (Scott; James.)

BANNER Mill. *See Martin & Leach* (76).

BARRETT, C. R. *See Pray* (96).

BARROW, Chas. W. *See Sproul, Deming & Emery* (119).

BERG. *See Schock & Berg* (106).

6* **BLACK, and S. H. Simonds.** E. of Floriston. Op. 1894– 98. Holdings in Nevada and California, incl. some in T18N R18E and in T17N R18E. (Grignon; Nevada.)

BLISS, D. L. *See Pray* (96); *Spooner* (117); *Woodburn* (143); *Yerington & Bliss* (144).

BOCA Mill & Ice Co. *See Akin et al* (1).

7. **BONI, Leon (Boney), and Wm. Jackman.** Near 1st Dog Valley Summit, CA, 4 mi. from Verdi, NV. Op. 1909–1926. Sawdust just W. of the summit marked the site in the 1930s. Cut 3 or 4 million ft. Logged with horses. (Mitchell; TT 8-15-1920; Mosconi).

BOSTON Mill. *See Leavitt* (64).

BOWKER. *See Higgins* (50).

8. **BRAGG Bros., Charles A. and Albert, and Gilman N. Folsom** (all Maine lumbermen). Central Mill, 1st mill site. At Little Bangor, 1½ mi. S. of Franktown, NV. In W½ of NW¼ of Sec. 15, T16N R19E. Op. 1861–70. (GLO 1862 T16N R19E; Bragg; Ratay.)

BRAGG, Charles Allen. *See Thomas R. Jones* (60).

BRAGG, Capt. *See Pray* (96).

9. **BRICKELL, E. J., and George Geisendorfer,** 1867–72; and **W. H. Kruger,** 1873–1909. 1st mill site of Truckee Lumber Co. Across river from Truckee. Waterpowered till 1871, then steampowered with 4 saws & daily cut of 50,000 ft. in 12 hours. Burned in 1903 and replaced with Yerington & Bliss Glenbrook mill. Holdings near Truckee of 6320 acres incl. Sec. 21, 27, 29, 33, ½ of 32, ¾ of 28, and 400 acres of Sec. 15 in T16N R17E; also incl. Sec. 9, 15, 16, 21 in T16N R16E. Sold 4–8 million ft. of lumber per year in Utah and Nevada. Total of 15–25 million cut annually. In 1900s had 10 mi. of railroad and 2 narrow gauge locomotives. (MSP 8-5-1876; TR 9-1878; Adams; Edwards pp12, 22, 26.)

10. **BRICKELL, E. J., and W. H. Kruger.** 2nd mill site of Truckee Lumber Co. New mill 1 mi. W. of Donner Lake at Billy Mack's Flat. Op. 1904–09, when after 32 years of operation the last log was milled by this company in Truckee Basin holdings. (PCWI 10-15-1909.)

BROWN, E. D. *See Prince, Brown & Eager* (98).

BRUHNES, Adolph C. *See Porter, Mitchell & Bruhnes* (94, 95).

11. **BUNKER Mill.** On Franktown Creek, 3 mi. SW of Franktown NV. In extreme corner Sec. 20, T16N R18E. Op. 1871–75. (GLO 1862 T16N R19E; Ratay; Koerber.)

12* **BURKHART, Charles, and J. H. Bachelder and Robert Gracey.** (1st Gracey mill site.) Merrill Valley Lumber Co. In Merrill Valley. Op. 1901–07. Logged 3 sections of jeffrey pine in Jones & Merrill Valleys. Cut 30 million ft. total. Marketing done from Boca. (PCWI Apr. & Dec. 1901; Gracey.)

13. **CALDWELL (and Williams?).** In Thomas Canyon, NV in Sec. 28 or 29, T18N R19E. Op. 1860–69. One steampowered saw. Daily cut 26,000 ft. Burned in 1869. (GHDN 5-29-1865; GLO 1867 T18N R19E; Koerber.)

CAMPBELL. *See Thompson, Clark & Campbell* (124).

CARSON & TAHOE Lumber & Flume Co. *See Pray* (96); *Yerington & Bliss* (144).

14. **CASNELL.** On Sugar Pine Point, Lake Tahoe, in Sec. 8, T14N R17E. Op. 1865–77. Steampowered. Casnell had 900 acres of timber on lakeshore between McKinney Creek and Sugar Pine Point. According to E. B. Scott, "Casnell" was a distortion of "Augustus Colwell" and was inscribed and perpeturated on GLO plat in 1865. (CDA 8-6-1868; Scott; GLO 1865 T19N R16E.)

15. **CELIO, C. G., and Sons.** 1st mill site 5 mi. S. of Meyers Station. 1 mi. S. of Celio Ranch. Op. 1910–27. Cut half a million ft. per year at steampowered mill with double circular saws. The elder Celio was a Swiss native. (Scott; EDR 6-11-1915; Greuner.)

16. **CELIO and Sons.** 2nd mill site. Half way between Meyers Station and Fallen Leaf Lake in Sec. 18, T12N R18E. Op. 1927–52. The Celios were in the lumber business for 47 years. (Scott; TT Sept. 1927.)

CENTRAL Mill. *See Bragg Bros.* (8).

17* **CHAPIN, Samuel A.** Above Alford's mill on Galena Creek, NV. Op. 1861–?. Employed 15 hands. Land included purchases of 4800 acres from Sierra Lumber & Mining Co. for $10,000. Waterpowered saw cut 15,000 ft. daily. (MSP 1-11-1862; Kelly 63.)

18. **CHEDIC, Geo. W., and D. B. Milne.** Coyote Mill. On Clear Creek, NV in SE¼ of Sec. 35, T15N R19E. Op. 1861–63, and by S. B. Martin from 1863–67. Waterpowered. Holdings incl. 498 acres purchased from Wm. R. Sears. (Angel pp541–42; GLO 1865 T15N R19E; Douglas.)

CLARK. *See Thompson & Clark & Campbell* (124).

COLWELL, Augustus. *See Casnell* (14).

COMANCHE Mill. *See Morton* (85a).

COMSTOCK. *See Lawrence & Comstock* (63).

COYOTE Mill. *See Chedic* (18).

CROWN-COLUMBIA. *See Floriston Pulp & Paper Co.* (34).

CROWN-WILLAMETTE. *See Floriston Pulp & Paper Co.* (34).

CRYSTAL PEAK Lumber Co. *See Hamlin, Meacham & McInstosh* (45).

CRYSTAL PEAK Shingle Factory. *See Ward & Fletcher* (137).

19. **DAVIES.** In Sardine Valley, Sec. 12, T19N R16E. Op. 1865. (GLO 1865 T19N R16E.)

20. **DAVIES, Llewellyn, and Sons.** 1st mill site? At Truckee. Op. 1901–? Cut about 3 million ft. per year. Possibly same family as the Davies in Sardine Valley much earlier. (Knowles.)

21* **DAVIES, Llewellyn, and Sons**. 2nd mill site. On Alder Creek. Op. 1901–02. (Knowles.)

22. **DAVIES Sons**. 3rd mill site. After father's death. At E. end of Donner Lake. Op. 1903–04. Bought and cut 25 million ft. at W. end of lake. Towed logs to mill. (Knowles.)

23* **DAVIES Sons**. 4th mill site. In Martis Valley near Truckee. Op. 1905–? Holdings incl. those deeded to company by L. Davies' widow in 1903: NW¼ Sec. 15 and N½ Sec. 16 T17N R17E. Planing mill and main office in Truckee. (Knowles; Nevada.)

24. **DAVIES Box & Lumber Co**. 5th mill site. At Davies spur in Sardine Valley, 11 mi. N. of Boca. Op. 1905–15. Logged the 100 million ft. in the Charles Mitchel stand. Moved the mill out of Truckee Basin to Blairsden in 1916. (Knowles; TR 10-11-1905; PCWI Nov. 1905.)

DAVIS, Charlton. *See Sproul, Deming & Emery* (119).

DAVIS & Son. *See Goff* (38).

DEMING, Theo. *See Sproul, Deming & Emery* (119).

DENIO, A. *See Negus & Lonkey* (68).

DENTON, Reuben. *See Jones & Denton* (59).

DIMMICK. *See Thomas & Dimmick* (123).

25. **DIXON, John**; owner of Yuba Mill. In Sec. 7, T19N R18E in Dog Valley on N. bank of stream. Op. 1862–79 by William & Fagan. Holdings incl. 1011 acres purchased from Joseph Walton in June 1864 by Dixon for $3000. Half interest in mill and land sold in April 1866 by John Dixon to Joseph Dixon for $5000. Waterpowered saw cut 10,000 ft. per day. Mill burned and rebuilt in 1862 and 1869. (MM 8-6-1862; Sierra; GLO 1865 T19N R18E; Goodwin p21.)

DIXON, Joseph. *See John Dixon* (25).

DOAN, Latimer E. *See Akin et al* (1).

DOANE. *See Hamlin & Doane* (44).

25a* **DONNER Boom & Lumber Co**. Fuelwood producer. Hq. probably near NE corner of Donner Lake. Maintained and operated splash dams on Truckee River. Charged fee for use in 1870s. Had contract for 10,000 cords in 1877. (Angel p282; Lord p351.)

26* **DYER**. In Little Valley. Op. 1871. (PCBD 1871 p133.)

EAGER. *See Prince, Brown & Eager* (98).

27* **EAGLE Mill**. Above Washoe City, NV. Op. 1867. (MSP 8-10-1867.)

28. **EASTMAN, C. H., and W. D. White**. 4 mi. W. of Glendale, NV (formerly Stone & Gates Crossing of Truckee River). Probably in Sec. 17, T19N R20E. Op. 1865–76. Holdings incl. land embracing large slough and dam reputedly purchased by Eastman & White in Jan. 1868 from Wm. R. Steele for $500. (SFB 6-7-1865; Washoe.)

ECLIPSE Mill. *See Thomas & Dimmick* (123).

EDWARDS. *See Saxton* (105).

ELKHORN Mill. *See Prince, Brown & Eager* (98).

29. **ELLEN, Elle**. His 1st mill site. At N. edge of Truckee. Op. 1868–77. Holdings incl. NW¼ Sec. 6, T17N R16E from H. Krisher in Oct. 1873; NW¼ Sec. 8, T17N R16E from John Robinson in Sept. 1874; SE¼ Sec. 6,

T17N R16E from J. V. Hoag in Jan. 1875. Cut 3 million ft. per year. (MSP 8-5-1876; Wells p168; Nevada.)

30. **ELLEN, Elle.** His 2nd mill site. 3 mi. from Truckee, on Trout Creek. Op. 1876–83. Holdings in T17N R16E incl. half interest in SW¼ Sec. 6 from A. J. Graham; NE¼ Sec. 8 from D. Parks government claim. Daily cut 40,000 ft. Flumed from mill to CPRR in Truckee. (MSP 8-5-1876; Nevada.)

ELLEN, Elle. His 3rd mill site. *See A. Proctor* (100).

ELLIOTT. *See Lewis* (66).

31. **ELLIOTT Bros.** (George, Thomas, John, and William Elliott). Summit Mill. Approx. 1 mi. E. of Glenbrook Summit, on Clear Creek in Douglas County, NV. In Sec. 6, T14N R19E. Op. 1863–72. Steampowered, 2 saws. Cut 15,000–30,000 ft. daily. Flumed lumber 10 mi. to Carson City. Bought by Carson Tahoe Lumber & Flume Co. (Yerington & Bliss) in 1872. They ran mill until 1875. (Angel pp541–42; Scott; Washoe; Koerber.)

EMERY, Joshua. *See Sproul, Deming & Emery* (119).

ESSEX Mill. *See Foulks* (35).

EXCELSIOR Mill. *See Goshen & Sproul* (39); *Hobart & Marlette* (51).

FAGAN. *See Dixon* (25).

FAIR, James. *See Higgins* (50); *Mackay & Fair* (73, 74).

32* **FALLEN LEAF Mill.** At Fallen Leaf Lake. Op. 1915. (EDR 6-11- 1915.)

FERGUSON, R. P. *See Hale, Thompson & Ferguson* (42, 43).

33* **FLANIGAN, P. L.** Located high up in Hunter Canyon. Op. during 1900s to 1912. Flumed lumber down Hunter Creek. (Knowles.)

FLETCHER. *See Ward & Fletcher* (137).

34. **FLORISTON Pulp & Paper Co.** At Floriston. Built in 1899. Op. from 1900 for 30 years on 24-hour day, 7 days a week. Center of logging operations was Duffy Camp until 1914, when contracted to log fir on 2000 acres of Truckee Lumber Co. lands. In 1921 shifted logging to Stanford, 2 mi. S. of Donner Lake. Tramway carried buckets of wood to railroad, thence to mill. Each bucket carried half cord of wood. Tram could operate over 10 ft. of snow. In 1922 purchased 3500 acres of Richardsons' land in Placer County. During 1923–26 about 10,000 cords per year was delivered to Floriston by Hobarts. At Duffy Camp operations logs generally cut in Oct. to season for 8 or 9 months. Trees cut down to 12 in. dia. to 4 or 6 in. top dia. Many stumps as high as 6 ft. due to logging over snow. In 1912 control of outfit went to Crown-Columbia. In 1914 known as Crown-Willamette. Had several miles of railroad in 1920s. (TT Jan 1921, Mar 1922; Schmidt; Adams.)

FOLSOM, Gilman N. *See Bragg Bros.* (8); *Thomas R. Jones* (60).

FOREST Mill. *See Thompson & Clark & Campbell* (124).

35. **FOULKES, John P., and George Foulkes.** Essex Mill. 1 mi. above Verdi, NV on Truckee River. Op. 1875–86. Sold to Hamlin & Doane in 1882 who ran it till 1886. A dam and flume were washed out in winter of 1875. Holdings in T19N R18E incl. 197 acres in Sec. 30 and 158 acres in Sec. 19; also in T19N R17E incl. 146 acres in Sec. 4 and 160 acres in Sec. 2. Used overshot waterwheel 1875–81 and waterdriven turbine 1881–86. Used animals for haul to log chutes. John Foulkes formerly ran the Snug Saloon

in the town of Crystal Peak. (Sierra; Hamlin; Goodwin pp33–35.)

36. **FOULKES, John P**. About half mi. east of 2nd Dog Valley Summit at Ingram Stage Station on old Donner-Henness Pass Road. Op. 1883–(90?). Skidded logs along skidways using horses. Also used team and wagon to transport lumber to Verdi, NV. (SVL 5-7-1883; Goodwin p33.)

37* **GAGE, Steve**. On Clear Creek. Op 1863. (Davis.)
GEISENDORFER, George. *See Brickell* (9).
GLENBROOK Mill Co. *See Goff* (38).

38. **GOFF, G. H. F., and George Merrill (later Davis & Son)**. At Glenbrook, NV, N. of wharf. Op. 1864–75. In late 1870s became property of Wells Fargo. Steampowered circular saw. Burned and rebuilt in 1869? (Angel pp372–81; Scott.)

39* **GOSHEN & SPROUL**. Excelsior Mill. Near town of Crystal Peak, west of Verdi, NV. Op. 1864–68. (Smith; GHDN 1-7-1865.)

40. **GRACEY, Robert G**. 2nd mill site. On Deep Creek, 1½ mi. from junction with Truckee River. Op. 1917–18. This was mill formerly abandoned by unidentified owner in Euer Valley. Daily capacity 30,000 ft. Total cut 4 or 5 million, mainly fir. Steampowered circular saw. Lumber flumed to Tahoe RR for transport to Floriston Paper Co. (TT 8-15-1917.)
GRACEY, Robert G. *See Burkhart, Bachelder & Gracey* (12).

40a **GRAY, Joseph**. His 2nd mill site. At Camp 20 on Truckee River, 2 mi. above Floriston. Op. 1872–80. Daily cut 30,000 ft. (CIT 12-25-1877.)
GRAY, Joseph. *See Shaffer & Gray* (108).

41. **GREGORY, Henry, and James Riddle**. 2½ mi. W. of Carson City, NV on Mill Creek (now Ash Creek). Op. from Fall 1859. Sold to James M. Thompson and Leonard L. Treadwell in 1862. 1st steampowered mill in Nevada. Daily cut 15,000 ft. (Angel pp541, 546; Washoe.)
GREY. *See Haskell & Grey* (46).

42. **HALE, Horace, and Jesse Thompson and R. P. Ferguson**. Pacific Shingle Co. 1st mill site. At Camp 16, 7 mi. below Truckee on river. Op. 1874–82. Offshoot of Nevada Ice Co. Waterpowered. Produced 5–10 million shingles per year. (Wells p168; TR 1-15-1874.)

43. **HALE, Horace, and Jesse Thompson and R. P. Ferguson**. Pacific Shingle Co. 2nd mill site. At Verdi, NV. Op. June 1875–? This was mill of Martin & Sweeney that was moved from mouth of Prosser Creek. (TR 8-4-1874.)
HALL. *See Seth Martin & Hall* (75).
HALL. *See Larrity & Hall & Revert* (62).

44. **HAMLIN, S. A., and Doane**. Stateline Mill. 5 mi. upriver from Essex, 6 mi. from Verdi. Just below Canyon 23–24 flats on flat adjacent to railroad bridge. Op. 1886–1900. Used horses, oxen and chutes at main logging from Lynham Camp. Cut about 3 million ft. annually at steampowered mill. Possibly Foster was also partner. (Hamlin.)

45. **HAMLIN, S. A., and R. S. Meacham and Alexander McIntosh**. Crystal Peak Lumber Co. in Dog Valley. (In E. part of Sec. 24, T20N R17E?) Op. 1876–79. Holdings in T20N R17E, incl. NE¼ and SE¼ of Sec. 14, NE¼ of Sec. 22 and NW¼ of Sec. 15. Mill sold to Patrick Henry and Frederick Katz in 1879. Op. till 1883, when sold to Truckee Lumber Co. (2nd TLC

mill). Op. till 1889. Annual cut 4–6 million ft. Had 5 mi. V flume to Verdi, NV. (Sierra; TR 3-7- 1881, 10-28-1882; Goodwin pp22–23.)

46. **HASKELL & GREY**. Subsequently Howe, Grey & Co. In Sec. 3, T14N R19E on Clear Creek, NV. Op. 1861–62. Waterpowered. (Angel pp541–42; GLO 1861 T14N R19E; Koerber.)

HATTERY, A. *See Alford* (2).

47* **HAWTHORNE, Wm. A**. 1st mill site. At Hawthorne Station in Lake Valley. Op. 1856–59. First mill in California part of basin. Eventually Hawthorne settled at Walker Lake, NV, where town of Hawthorne was named for him. Possibly this mill was sited about 1 mi. E. of the Sierra House. See an unidentified mill reported at that location on Cold Creek. (Wren.)

48* **HAWTHORNE, Wm. A**. 2nd mill site. On Martis Creek. Op. 1860s? (Wren.)

49* **HAWTHORNE, Wm. A.** 3rd mill site. At Webber Lake. Op. 1860s? (Wren.)

HAYNIE, J. W. *See Lonkey* (69).

HEATON. *See Munger & Starbuck* (86).

HEATON. *See A. H. Wilson* (142).

HENRY, Patrick. *See Hamlin, Meacham & McIntosh* (45).

50* **HIGGINS**. On Hunter Creek. Op. began 1871. Bought by J. J. Poor & Bowker for $500 in 1872. Daily cut 8000 ft. One waterpowered saw. Reported operated by Mackay & Fair in 1876. Thus, their first, larger steampowered mill may have been built on same site. (PCBD 1871 p133; Washoe.)

51* **HOBART, Walter S., and Samuel H. Marlette**. 1st mill site. Excelsior Mill. In Little Valley, 4 mi. W. of Mill Station. Op. 1873–78. Two steampowered saws. Daily cut 25,000 ft. (PCBD 1876; RG 11-3-1879; Washoe.)

52* **HOBART, Walter S., and S. H. Marlette**. 2nd mill site. Possibly located at head of Hobart's Ravine in Sec. 17, T15N R19E. Ravine shown on National Forest map. Op. 1878–?. (RG 11-3-1879; Koerber.)

53. **HOBART, W. S., and S. H. Marlette**. 3rd mill site. Incline Mill. On Mill Creek at Incline, NV, ½ mi. from N. shore, Lake Tahoe. Op. 1879–93. Served by a narrow gauge double track tramline, 4000 ft. long, with lift of 1400 ft. to V flume that carried lumber and cordwood through tunnel and then to Lakeview on V&TRR. Company employed 250 men at peak operation. Rafted many logs to Incline from south Tahoe using steamer *Niagara* to tow. Owned thousands of acres of timberland adjacent to the lake. (RG 11-3-1879; Scott; James p204; Koerber.)

54. **HOBART, W. S., and S. H. Marlette**. 4th mill site. Sierra Nevada Wood & Lumber Co. At Hobart Mills, 7 mi. N. of Truckee. Op. Sept. 1895 to 1936. Head saws were: band, 52 in. double circular, 36 in. gang. By 1912 holdings were mainly in vicinity of Little Truckee River, totaling 65,650 acres; about half cutover and half virgin timberland. Some holdings purchased about 2 decades prior to harvest—e.g., 80 acres in Sec. 22 T17N R15E bought by Marlette in 1879 for $1 per acre. Cut 1 billion ft. total at 5 locations. One of first outfits in basin to purchase national forest timber.

In 1922 logged with Willamette donkeys, in 1928 with Caterpillars. (Sierra; AL 10-14-1899; CBF.)

55* **HOBART, W. S., and S. H. Marlette.** 5th mill site. Hobart's Alder Creek Mill. On Alder Creek, 2 mi. below Davies Mill. Op. 1901. Daily capacity 20,000 to 30,000 ft. Hauled lumber to railroad with teams. (CBF.)

HOBART Mills. *See Hobart & Marlette* (54).

HOWE. *See Haskell & Grey* (46).

56* **HUGHES, F. J.** Monitor Mill. In Kings Canyon. Op. 1863–66. (Washoe; Angel pp541–42.)

57. **HYDE, Elder Orson.** Half mi. W. of Franktown, NV. Op. Nov. 1856 by Hyde; 1857–62 by Jacob Rose and R. D. Sides. 1st mill in Nevada part of basin. 2 saws, circular and upright. (Angel p623; Ratay; GLO 1862 T16N R19E.)

58* **HYMER, Thomas K.** Near Washoe City, NV. Op. 1860–68. Possibly this mill was in Galena or in Thomas Canyon; even possible Hymer had mills in both localities. (Wren.)

INCLINE Mill. *See Hobart & Marlette* (53).

JACKMAN, Wm. *See Boni & Jackman* (7).

59* **JONES, Charles, and Reuben Denton.** In Clear Creek vicinity. Op. 1861–63. Also produced shingles. Steampowered. W. Allen had ¼ interest in mill and timber section that he sold to Jones & Denton in June 1861. (Angel p541; Wells; Douglas.)

60. **JONES, Thomas R.** At Clinton (Camp 18, Now Hirschdale). Op. 1868–70. In 1st year of operation cut 16 million ft. One of largest producers in region. Sold mill to Chas. A. Bragg and Gilman Folsom (Pacific Wood & Lumber Co.) in 1870. Their daily cut of 45,000 ft. (at this, their 2nd millsite) came from holdings in T16N R16E and T16N R17E totaling 6320 acres. They sold 4–8 million ft. annually in Utah and Nevada from total of 15–25 million annual cut. In 1878 began using first steam loco. in Truckee area with 6 mi. of narrow gauge track and 2 locos. Prior to 1878 the company used to drive Prosser Creek, Little Truckee and main river for log transport. The mill (2nd Bragg & Folsom site) burned and was rebuilt several times: in 1873, 1878, and 1889. Operations ceased in 1894. Jones may have built another mill at this locality. This was apparently called Burkhalter mill after man who built RR up nearby Juniper Creek. (MSP 8-5-1876; CDA July 1873; Adams.)

KATZ, Frederick. *See Hamlin Meacham & McIntosh* (45).

60a **KIDDER Bros.** Mill near Bronco. Op. 1891–92. Flumed lumber to Bronco, to RR. Mason possibly was a partner. (Knowles p40.)

KLEIN, Jacob. *See Wagner & Klein* (135).

KNEELAND, John. *See Stanford* (120).

61. **KNOX, J. R.** About 1½ mi. W. of Lakeview NV. Op. 1864–67 and later. Possibly James H. Rigby was a partner in 1870. Holdings incl. timberland in SW¼ Sec. 28, T16N R19E purchased for $1400 by J. R. Knox from L. Lilly in Jan. '73. (Knowles p11; Washoe; Ratay.)

KRUGER, W. H. *See Brickell & Geisendorfer & Kruger* (9); *Brickell & Kruger* (10).

LAKE BIGLER Lumber Co. *See Pray* (96).

62* **LARRITY & HALL and Al Revert**. On N. side of Dog Valley. Op. 1896–1902. Logged with horses and Dolbeer donkeys. Steam powered circular mill saw. In 1898 an old mill boiler salvaged from Snodgrass operation blew up, killing James Sherrick, an engineer. Logged 3 million ft. east of Crystal Peak. (Casey; Mosconi; Goodwin p37; REG 10-6-1898.)

63* **LAWRENCE & COMSTOCK**. Near Tallac. Op. early 1900s. One of first electric mills in the basin, generating power from Tailor Creek, a mile away. Daily cut 25,000 ft. In 1909 employed 150 men. (PCWI 7-1-1909.)

LEACH. *See Martin & Leach* (76).

64. **LEAVITT, Ben H**. Boston Mill. At Dog Valley Summit, W. side of Truckee turnpike. Op. 1860 to Dec. 1867, when Leavitt's interest, including 320 acres of timberland, was sold to B. S. Southern. (Smith; REG 7-24-1915; Sierra.)

65* **LEBROKE, Thomas**. Mill in Webber Canyon, 6 mi. from Webber Lake. Op. 1887. Hauled lumber 16 mi. to Meadow Lake. (TR 3-2-1887.)

65a **LEWERS**. 2½ mi. NW of Lakeview NV on Lewers Creek. Op. 1860s. Steam powered. (Ratay.)

66. **LEWIS & ELLIOTT**. 3 mi. S. of Franktown NV. In SW¼ of Sec. 22, T16N R19E. Op. 1862. (GLO 1862 T16N R19E.)

LEWISON, J. L. *See David Smith & Lewison* (112).

67. **LOCKE, John**. Probably in Sec. 31, T13N R18E, El Dorado Co., CA. Op. began 1874 or 1875. Sold with much land in both CA and NV to Michele Spooner & "Red" Patton for $25,000. This was the 3rd Spooner millsite. Some records indicate that "Locke" may have been John "Lonkey," brother of Oliver, and that the Lonkeys were active for a time in the Clear Creek-Spooner Summit area. (TR 6-2-1875; PCBD 1876 pp587,598; Douglas; Goodwin pp50–51.)

68. **LONKEY, Oliver, and T. G. Negus**. Also partners for brief periods were A. Denio, Montrose & Stage. 1st Lonkey mill site by this outstanding lumberman of French-Canadian birth. Mill SW of Ophir NV in NW¼ of Sec. 8, T16N R19E. Op. 1862–68. Land purchases incl. part of "Watson Claim," 560 acres of "Parker Claim," part of "Perkins & Hammond ranches." Hammond ranch, purchased in 1866, was reported to include a sawmill. (Kelly 1863; GLO 1862 T16N R19E; Washoe; Ratay; Koerber.)

69. **LONKEY, Oliver, and T. G. Negus**. 2nd Lonkey mill site. In Little Valley NV, probably in S½ of Sec. 8, T16N R19E. They operated 1869–1872, when purchased by J. W. Haynie, Yerington & Ralston. They operated 1872–1878? Flumed output to Franktown NV. Possibly this mill operated first by Woodward & Hammond. (Kelly 63; Washoe; Ratay; Koerber.)

70* **LONKEY, Oliver, and E. R. Smith**. 5th Lonkey mill site. (Verdi Mill Co., Dog Valley Mill). In Dog Valley. Op. 1880s to 1915. Had standard gauge RR for terrain between Dog Valley and Merrill Creek, partly horses, partly donkey logging for timber purchased from Truckee Lumber Co. Hauled lumber to Verdi with tricycle steam wagons. (REG 7-24-1915; Hamlin; AL 11-2-1918; Sierra.)

71. **LONKEY, Oliver**. 6th Lonkey mill site. Verdi Lumber Co. On west end of

Verdi NV. Today abandoned log pond marks the mill site. Op. 1900 to May 1926, when mill burned. Up-to-date steam plant with bandsaw. Capacity 40,000 ft. daily. Prior to 1910 used horses and Dolbeers for clearcuts in Dog Valley; later used bull donkey yarders. Company was one of first taking advantage of "long-term" contracts initiated by the Forest Service. In 1911 contracted to cut 10 million ft. of government timber over a 10 year period. Cut approx. 12,000 ft. per acre, mostly ponderosa pine, on own holdings. Built standard gauge RR into Dog Valley for log hauls to Verdi. Large planing mill and box factory were also sited at Verdi. (Casey; REB 4-10-1914; JRP p142; Goodwin pp85,86,100; Myrick.)

LONKEY, Oliver. *See Martin & Hall for this 3rd Lonkey mill site* (75); *Martin & Leach* (76).

72* **LOOMIS, George**. In White's Canyon. Op. 1860–62. (Kelly 62.)

MACHOMICK, James. *See A. Proctor* (100).

MACKAY, John. *See Higgins* (50).

73. **MACKAY, John, and James Fair**. 1st mill site. Pacific Wood, Lumber & Flume Co. On Hunter Creek (at Hunter Lake, NV). Op. 1874–77. Daily cut 25,000 ft. Flumed lumber 15 mi. to Huffaker's Station on V&TRR. (Bancroft pp288–290.)

74. **MACKAY, John, and James Fair**. 2nd mill site. Pacific Wood, Lumber & Flume Co. On Middle Fork of Evans Creek NV. Op. 1875–80. Flumed to Huffaker's Station on V&TRR, over flume originating at Hunter's Creek mill and serving both mills. At peak, 800 men were employed cutting, sawing and fluming to serve both mills. Another 120 (all Chinese) piled and loaded wood at Huffaker's. Daily cut 70,000 ft. Payroll $81,000 per month. Forests were denuded since trees not suitable for logs were taken out as cordwood. (Bancroft pp288–290.)

74a* **MARKER Bros. Hans and Pete**. Cordwood producers. On Galena Creek. Op. 1872–Dec. 1881. Flumed to Washoe City. From there hauled wood to Virginia City. Produced 10–15,000 cords annually. Markers were emigrants from Copenhagen. (Gregory; Knowles p25.)

MARLETTE, Samuel H. *See Hobart & Marlette* (51).

MARLETTE, S. H. *See Hobart & Marlette* (52, 53, 54, 55).

MARLICK. *See Reed, Marlick & Co.* (101).

MARTIN, S. B. *See Chedic* (18).

75. **MARTIN, Seth, and Hall**. Built mill in 1872. Sold in 1873 to Nevada & California Lumber Co. (Oliver Lonkey & E. Smith). 3rd Lonkey mill site. Op. 1873–80. Mill on Prosser Creek 6 mi. from Truckee in Sec. 21, T18N R16E. Waterpowered turbine. Daily cut 30,000 ft. Flumed output 5½ mi. to Prosser Cr. Station on CPRR. Supplied sash and door factory at Camp 16 and factory and planing mill at Verdi. Holdings of Nevada & California Lumber Co. of 1760 acres incl. ¼ Sec. 16, all Sec. 20, all Sec. 21, all Sec 7 in T18N R16E. Cost of Sec. 7 in 1875 from CPRR was $5 per acre. (MSP 8-5-1876; TR 8-3- 1872; Nevada.)

76. **MARTIN & LEACH**. Banner Mill. 8 mi. from Truckee on Sage Hen Creek, where the RR crossed it. Op. 1874–82. By Lonkey & E. R. Smith

from 1882–89. Daily cut per 12 hr. day, 100,000 ft. 4th Lonkey mill site. (MSP 8-5- 1876.)

77. **MARTIN, Seth, and Sweeney**. Shingle mill at mouth of Prosser Creek. Possibly Hall was also partner. Op. 1874. (TR 8-4-1874.)

MARYSVILLE Mill. *See D. Arnold* (3).

MAYFLOWER Mill. *See Prince, Brown & Eager* (98).

78. **McFARLAND, Samuel**. His 1st mill site. On NW edge of Washoe (Lake) City NV. Op. 1862–63, possibly till 1875. Steam powered. (BL; Map 1-847 W2 1862 B2; Gregory; Washoe.)

79. **McFARLAND, Samuel**. His 2nd mill site. On Brown's Creek 3 mi. S. of Galena NV. In S. half of Sec. 21, T17N R19E. Op. 1867. One steampowered saw cut 10,000 ft. per day. (GLO 1867 T17N R19E; PCBD 1867 p46; Ratay; Koerber.)

80. **McFARLAND, Samuel**. His 3rd mill site. On Truckee River, just above mouth of Little Truckee. Op. 1867–72. Two steampowered saws. Daily cut 20,000 ft. (Lord p8 map.)

81* **McFARLAND, Samuel**. His 4th mill site. On S. fork of Martis Creek, 4 mi. from Truckee. Location approximate. Op. 1872–80. Three steampowered saws. Flumed lumber to RR over flume of Sisson, Wallace & Co. (TR 6-22-1872.)

McINTOSH, Alexander. *See Hamlin, Meacham & McIntosh* (45).

82. **McKAY, Stewart, and J. A. Stewart**. McKay's 1st mill site. In Union Valley. Op. 1891–96. Holdings in T17N R17E incl. W½ of Sec. 3 in 1888 from CPRR for $1400 and ½ of Sec. 4 in 1892. (Knowles p41; Nevada.)

83* **McKAY, Stewart**. His 2nd mill site. He bought out partner J. A. Stewart and moved mill from location near Union Mills to Sardine Valley. Op. 1897. Shipped lumber over 9 mi. of RR to Hobart Mills. (Knowles p41.)

84* **McMILLAN & WORN**. At Star, 3 mi. from Boca on Boca-Loyalton RR in Sierra Co.? Op. Aug. 1909 to Oct. 1913 when Mill burned. Cut 40,000 ft. daily. (Knowles p43.)

85. **McPHERSON, Angus**. Former SF resident. Mill ½ mi. SE of Donner Lake on Coldstream Creek. Op. 1864–69. Small waterpowered mill with two circular saws. Extensive holdings incl: Donner Lake property from Henry Arnold in Sept. 1863; King's Ranch property (Samuel King) along S. boundary of Donner Lake, in Dec. 1863; 1½ sq. mi. along both sides of Coldstream in Feb. 1864 from Jesse Baker; SE¼ Sec. 18, T17N R16E, plus another 160 acres from U.S. in 1869; ½ sq. mi. lying along Coldstream from Wm. Haskell in Sept. 1864 for $3,000 incl. mill. Much of McPherson holdings are now in the Donner Memorial Park. (Edwards pp21–26; Nevada.)

MEACHAM, R. S. *See Hamlin Meacham & McIntosh* (45).

MERRILL, George. *See Goff* (38).

MERRILL VALLEY Lumber Co. *See Burkhart, Bachelder & Gracey* (12).

MILLER, Andrew H. *See David G. Smith* (111).

MILLER. *See Munger & Starbuck* (86).

MILLER, George. *See A. H. Wilson* (142).

MILLS, D. O. *See Yerington & Bliss* (144).

MILNE, D. B. *See Chedic* (18).

MITCHELL. *See Porter & Mitchell* (93); *Porter, Mitchell & Bruhnes* (94,95).

MONITOR Mill. *See F. J. Hughes* (56).

MONTROSE. *See Lonkey* (68).

85a **MORTON**. Comanche Mill. On Winter's Creek NV. 3 mi. W. of Washoe City. Probably in NW corner Sec. 28, T17N R19E Op. 1867? (Ratay; Koerber.)

86* **MUNGER & STARBUCK**. Operating near Truckee. Op. 1868. Possibly Miller & Heaton were also partners. (Wells.)

87. **MUSGROVE, W. R**. 2½ mi. S. of Franktown NV, in NW¼ of Sec. 22, T16N R19E. Op. 1862–67. Holdings incl. lands purchased in June 1865 in Secs. 29 and 32, T16N R19E, totaling 480 acres. Mill moved to Little Valley in 1867? (GLO 1862 T16N R19E; MA 6-28-1877; Washoe; Ratay.)

NEGUS, T. G. *See Lonkey* (68,69).

NEVADA & CALIFORNIA Lumber Co. *See Martin & Hall* (75).

88* **NICHOLS, H. O**. On Webber Creek. Op. 1907. Cut National Forest timber. (PCWI July 1907.)

89* **NORCROSS, Thomas**. At or near Glendale. Op. 1860–63? (Angel; WCES 8-31-1867.)

90. **OPHIR Mill**. At Ophir NV. Op. 1861–64. Employed a hundred men in wood cutting and the sawmill and more than that in the associated ore processing mill. (SFB 6-3-1861, 10-24-1861, 10-30-1862; MSP 2-27-1877.)

PACIFIC Shingle Co. *See Hale, Thompson & Ferguson* (42,43).

PACIFIC Wood & Lumber Co. *See Thomas R. Jones* (60).

PACIFIC Wood, Lumber & Flume Co. *See Mackay & Fair* (73,74).

91* **PARSONS Bros., Nathan and Jay**. Near Sardine House in head of Sardine Valley, on Henness Pass turnpike between Jordan and Ingraham Stations. Op. 1866–72? Waterpowered mill with daily capacity of 8,000 ft. Later converted to steam. Sold in 1866 to Wm. A. Slack for $600. Known also as Parsons & Welch mill. (PCBD 1871; Sierra; Jackson p45.)

PATTON. *See John Locke* (67).

92. **PERSON, Acey** (Asa?). West of town of Galena NV, at SE corner of Sec. 5, T17N R19E. Op. 1860–63. Daily cut 26,000 ft. running day and night. Sold lumber for $35–50 per MBM. (MSP 1-11-1862; GLO 1865 T17N R19E; Koerber.)

PERSON, Asa (Acey?) *See Alford* (2).

POOR, J. J. *See Higgins* (50).

93* **PORTER & MITCHELL**. 1st mill site. Sunrise Mill. Just south of town of Crystal Peak. Possibly sited on flat just W. of jct. of Sunrise Basin Road and foot of Dog Valley grade. Op. 1897–1902. Cut 15 million ft. off Sec. 36. Operated with horses, Dolbeers and chutes from May-Nov each year. Daily cut 20,000 ft. plus. (Porter; Mosconi; Goodwin p10.)

94* **PORTER & MITCHELL & Adolf C. Bruhnes**. 2nd mill site. Sunrise Mill. At Pine on Boca-Loyalton RR, 4 mi. N. of Boca. Op. 1902–07. This mill moved from Crystal Peak and a new partner, Adolf C. Bruhnes, joined the firm. Logging was with Dolbeers and chutes. Cut 12–15 million from 2½ sections incl. 160 acres in E. part of Sec. 34, T19N R17E. (Porter; Sierra.)

95. **PORTER & MITCHELL & BRUHNES**. 3rd mill site. Sunrise Mill. Sited one mi. S. of mouth of Merrill Creek after being moved from Pine. Op. 1907. Cut and logged for one year, then mill sold to O. M. Ward & Bros. who operated 1908–12. Used Dolbeers. (Porter.)

96. **PRAY, A. W.** (lumberman from Maine). Lake Bigler Lumber Co. At Glenbrook NV, S. of wharf. Op. 1861–67 with partners C. R. Barrett and N. D. Winters. Pray sole owner in 1867. Reputedly used machinery of original Woodburn mill. Waterpowered with 2 saws, diameters 60 and 50 in. Converted to steam in 1864 at cost of $20,000. Daily cut 20,000 ft. Sold common lumber at $25 per M, clear at $45. Was the first to raft logs by steam tug across Lake Tahoe. Carson & Tahoe Lumber & Flume Co. (Yerington & Bliss) owned mill from 1873. Mill operator in 1875 was Capt. Bragg. (TR 6-2-1875; Scott pp380–381.)

97. **PRICE, Wm.** At foot of Slide Mtn. NV, on S. side of mountain. Probably in SW¼ Sec. 32, T17N R19E. Op. 1875–81. Had 1500 acres timberland incl. purchases in T16N R19E and T17N R18E. Remains of mill site evident in 1930s near Price Lake. (GHDN 7-29-1875; Washoe; Koerber.)

98. **PRINCE, Thomas B., and E. D. Brown and Eager**. Elkhorn (Mayflower?) Mill. 3 mi. SW of Steamboat Springs, 1½ mi. S. of Galena NV. One report suggests this mill (Brown's Mill) was owned by Matt Harbin & Co. Ratay's map shows "N.Y." mill approximately at this location. (MSP 1-11-1862; Kelly 63; SFH 2-13-1860; Washoe; Ratay.)

99* **PROCTOR (Daniel and Alexander)**. Near town of Crystal Peak. Op. 1864–68. Possibly Daniel Proctor had 4 mill sites in this vicinity. (Smith; GHDN 1-7-1865; CIT 12-25-1877.)

100. **PROCTOR, A**. Alder Creek Mill. About 2 mi. N. of Truckee in NE¼ of Sec. 34, T18N R16E. In Sept. 1869 Proctor sold to Charles E. Roberson & James Machomick. They cut until 1883. Then was operated by Elle Ellen (his 3rd mill site) until 1901. Had 2 circular saws, shingle machine and planing mill, all steampowered. Daily cut 40,000 ft. in 12 hours. Output about a million ft. annually during 1890s. Had 5 mi. of flume to RR at mouth of Prosser Creek. (TR 9-28-1872, 6-10-1873; Nevada.)

RALSTON. *See Lonkey* (69).

RAMSEY Mill. *See Alford* (2).

101. **REED, MARLICK & Co**. In Little Valley NV, in SW¼ of Sec. 17, T16N R19E. Op. 1862. (GLO 1862 T16N R19E; Ratay.)

REVERT. *See Larrity & Hall & Revert* (62).

102. **RICHARDSON Bros. (Warren and George)**. This, their 1st mill site, was on W. Middle Martis Creek 6 mi. from Truckee; E. of Shaffer's mill. Op. 1874–83. Holdings in T16N R17E, incl. 103 acres in Sec. 5 purchased from CPRR in Aug. 1871 for $653; also NW¼ of Sec. 5 purchased from J. Butler May 1877 for $600; also, in T17N R17E, SE¼ Sec. 32 purchased April 1878. Employed 35 men in woods and mill and 40 in box factory. Used flanged wheeled steam locos and flat cars on wooden rails for log transport. Flumed lumber 5½ mi. to planing mill and box factory at CPRR at mouth of Martis Creek below town of Truckee. Prior to 1874, mill was located at Summit Valley, west of Truckee Basin. (Edwards; MSP 8-5-1876; Placer.)

103. **RICHARDSON Bros**. This, their 2nd millsite, was near corner of Secs. 4 & 5, T16N R17E, and Secs. 32 & 33, T17N R17E, a few miles S. of their 1st mill site. Op. 1883–1906. Bought holdings in T16N R17E, incl. SW¼ Sec. 5 for $880 in Jan. 1880 and bought 160 acres in NE¼ of Sec 4 for $650 in Dec. 1882; bought NW¼ of Sec. 3 for $1207 in Feb. 1883; also NE¼ of Sec. 3 for $1209 in Oct. 1883. All from CPRR. Hauled lumber by steam wagon 8 mi. to yard and box factory in E. part of Truckee. (PCWI Feb. 1892; Placer; Richardson.)

RIDDLE, James. *See Gregory* (41).

RIDEOUT, J. R. *See D. Arnold* (3).

RIGBY, James H. *See Knox* (61).

ROBERSON, Charles. *See A. Proctor* (100).

ROSE, Jacob. *See Hyde* (57).

104. **SAMSON**. On W. side of Dog Valley grade. In Sec. 7, T19N R18E. Op. 1865. (GLO 1865 T19N R18E; Goodwin p10.)

105. **SAXTON, Augustus H., and Son, Reuben H**. On Tahoe's shore, N. of Ward Creek. In Sec. 13, T15N R16E. Op. 1863–77. 54 ft. overshot waterwheel was first power, then steam with 2 saws. Edwards was partner in 1881. Fire destroyed main Saxton timber stands in 1877. Mill site used as wood camp until 1887. (PCBD 1871; CDA 8-6-1868; Scott; GLO 1865 T15N R16E.)

106. **SCHOCK, Caspar, and Berg**. Shingle mill at Squaw Valley junction with the Truckee River. Op. 1875–80. Ran day and night. Waterpowered. (TR 5-6-1875.)

SCOFIELD, N. E. *See Smith & Scofield* (113,114).

SEARS, Wm. R. *See Chedic & Milne* (18).

107* **SHAFFER, George**. 1st mill site. On Clear Creek. Op. 1861–67. Probably located where Summit Mill was sited later. Two steampowered saws. Daily cut 8,000 ft. Moved mill to Truckee in 1867. (Wren p642; Edwards; Douglas.)

108. **SHAFFER, George H., and Jos. Gray**. Shaffer's 2nd mill site. Across river from and S. of Truckee. Op. 1867–71. (Edwards; Meschery p43.)

109. **SHAFFER, George**. 3rd mill site. In Martis Valley 3 mi. SE of Truckee on W. branch of Martis Creek. Op. 1871–82. Extensive holdings incl. all Sec. 2 T16N R16E. Purchased SW¼, NW¼ and SE¼ in Nov. 1873, and NE¼ for $800 in March 1875. Bought water rights to W. branch of Martis Cr., SW of mill, from Sisson, Wallace & Co. for $5,000 in July 1873. Bought Sec. 35, T17N R16E (640 acres) from CPRR for $4480 in Feb. 1876. Daily cut 35,000 ft. Main markets in Nevada and Utah. (Edwards; TR 5-2-1872, 8-3-1872; Placer.)

110. **SHAFFER, George**. 4th mill site. In NE corner Sec. 35, T17N R16E, on W. branch of Martis Creek. Op. 1883–Sept. 1905 when mill burned. By 1892 hauled logs with RR loco and 4 cars for 2 mi. between logging camp and mill. Lumber flumed 3 mi. to yards 1 mi. SE of Truckee. Daily cut 90,000 ft. In 1880s annual cut 3 million ft. plus. (PCWI Feb 1892; JRP; Ratay; Toiyabe.)

SHERMAN, C. P. *See Stevens & Sherman* (121).

SHERRITT, James. *See David G. Smith* (111).

SIDES, R. D. *See Hyde* (57).

SIERRA NEVADA Wood & Lumber Co. *See Hobart & Marlette* (54).

SILVER STATE Mill. *See Sproul, Deming & Emery* (119).

SIMONDS, S. H. *See Black & Simonds* (6).

110a* **SISSON, WALLACE & Co**. Fuelwood producer. Near Truckee. Also produced charcoal. In 1874 shipped weekly 1,000 to 2,000 bushels to Virginia City. Employed over 350 Chinese in charcoal production. Possibly largest fuelwood producer in the basin in 1870s. (Angel p282; Lord p351; Fahey p13.)

SLACK, Wm. A. *See Parsons Bros.* (91).

111. **SMITH, David G**. 1st mill site. Shingle mill 5 mi. from Truckee on road to Brockway. Op. 1880–83. Burned and rebuilt in 1880. Daily cut 40,000 shingles. Sold mill and holdings to James Sherritt & Andrew Miller in 1881 for $3,000. Holdings in Sec. 28, T17N R17E incl. NE¼, W½ of SE¼, and E½ of SW¼. (TR 7-17-1880; Placer.)

112. **SMITH, David, and J. L. Lewison**. Smith's 2nd mill site. On Coldstream. Op. 1887–98. Dam floated 700,000 ft. of logs. Flume took lumber and cordwood 1½ mi. to Stanford siding yards on CPRR. In 1902 contracted for delivery of 50,000 cords of 4-foot wood to Floriston—largest such contract in Truckee Basin. (TR 11-30-1887.)

SMITH, E. R. *See Lonkey & Smith* (70); *See Martin & Hall* (75,76).

113* **SMITH, I. A. (Winnie?), and N. E. Scofield**. 1st mill site. On Alder Creek. Op. 1899–1902. Holdings incl. Sec. 36, T18N R15E. Bought by Scofield from F. D. Hilton. (WCL 1917 pp94,95; Nevada; Mosconi.)

114* **SMITH, I. A. (Winnie? Ira?), and N. E. Scofield**. 2nd mill site. In Russel Valley. Op. 1902–17. Holdings incl. 160 acres in Sec. 32, T19N R17E, and 190 acres in SE¼ of Sec. 12, T18N R16E. (Jackson pp55–56; WCL 1917 pp94–95; Nevada; Sierra; Mosconi.)

115. **SMITH, I. A. (Winnie)**. His 3rd mill site. On Little Truckee River just above its junction with Sage Hen Creek. Op. 1915–? Smith may have had two mill sites in this locality. Reported to have rejected using RR of Sierra Nevada Wood & Lumber Co. to carry his lumber; instead hauled it to market with oxen. (Jackson pp55–56; Mosconi.)

116. **SNODGRASS, John**. Just west of first Dog Valley Summit. An old boiler and sawdust used to mark the location. Op. 1860–? Snodgrass was a prominent rancher with holdings S. of Reno. (Mitchell; REG 7-24-1915.)

SOUTHERN, B. S. *See Leavitt* (64).

117. **SPOONER, Michele E., and Co**. Shingle and saw mill. Near Spooner Station NV (jct. of present highways 50 and 28). The 1st mill site of this lumberman from Canada. Op. 1863–72. Bought by Yerington & Bliss in 1872. (Scott; Koerber.)

118. **SPOONER, Michele E**. His 2nd mill site. A new mill ½ mi. S. of Spooner Station NV in 1873. Bought by Yerington & Bliss and op. until 1875. (Scott; Koerber.)

SPOONER, Michele E. *See John Locke* (67).

119* **SPROUL, R., and Theo. Deming and Joshua Emery**. Silver State Mill.

Four mi. below Truckee on N. bank of river between Camps 18 and 19? At Stonewall Station? Op. 1867–69. Sold in 1867 to Charlton Davis, then in 1868 to Charles W. Barrow. Holdings incl. SW¼ of Sec. 35, T18N R17E. Mill burned in 1869. (TST 12-25-1869; Nevada.)

SPROUL. *See Goshen & Sproul* (39).

STAGE. *See Lonkey* (68).

120. **STANFORD, A. P.** SW of Truckee near headwaters of Coldstream Creek. Op. 1868–82. In latter part of period owned by John Kneeland. Daily cut 30,000 ft. (PCBD 1871.)

STARBUCK. *See Munger & Starbuck* (86).

STATELINE Mill. *See Hamlin & Doane* (44).

121. **STEVENS, W. F., and C. P. Sherman**. In a little valley near Lawton Hot Springs NV, harvested a stand of sugar pine. Op. 1912–? This mill was formerly Flanigan's and was moved from Hunter Creek. (REG 7-19-1912.)

STEWART, J. A. *See McKay & Stewart* (82).

STILTZ, George. *See Alford* (2).

122. **STOCKHAM**. On Franktown Creek a mile W. of Franktown NV. In NW¼ of NE¼ of Sec. 9, T16N R19E. Op. 1862–63. (GLO 1862 T16N R19E; GLO 1863 T16N R19E; Ratay; Koerber.)

SUMMIT Mill. *See Elliot Bros.* (31).

SUNRISE Mill. *See Porter & Mitchell* (93); *See Porter, Mitchell & Bruhnes* (94,95).

SWEENEY. *See Martin & Sweeney* (77).

123* **THOMAS & DIMMICK**. Eclipse Mill. In Thomas Canyon. Op. 1860– 65. (GHDN 5-29-1865.)

124* **THOMPSON & Clark & Campbell**. Forest Mill. Near Washoe City in Gold Canyon. Op. 1862–63. (Kelly 63.)

125. **THOMPSON, James M., and Leonard L. Treadwell**. On Mill Creek (now Ash Cr.) NV, 1 mi. N. of Gregory & Riddle mill site. Op. 1861–? Steam-powered. Daily cut 15,000 ft. Also associated shingle and planing mill. (Angel pp541–542.)

THOMPSON, Jesse. *See Hale, Thompson & Ferguson* (42,43).

126. **TOWLE Bros**. Mill sited close to RR on S. shore of Donner Lake. Op. 1867–71. 4 steampowered saws. Daily cut 100,000 ft. Prior to milling at Donner Lake these lumbermen, in 1858, were 1st mill owners at Dutch Flat on W. slope of Sierra. (Lardner; Adams.)

TREADWELL, Leonard L. *See James Thompson & Treadwell* (125).

TRUCKEE Lumber Co. *See Brickell & Geisendorfer & Kruger* (9); *See Brickell & Kruger* (10).

127. **UNIDENTIFIED owner**. On Evans Creek NV in SE¼ of Sec. 7, T18N R19E. Op. 1867–? (GLO 1867 T18N R19E.)

128. **UNIDENTIFIED owner**. One mi. E. of Sierra House in Lake Valley CA. Op. early 1860s. Waterpowered up and down saw. This mill site possibly is that of the Hawthorne mill, for which there is no specific reported location in Lake Valley. Also it is possible that the Woodburn mill was located here on Cold Creek, though more likely that mill was sited on Trout Creek. (Angel.)

129. **UNIDENTIFIED owner.** Shingle mill in Clear Creek NV drainage. In NW¼ of Sec. 34, T15N R19E. Op. 1865. (GLO 1865 T15N R19E.)

130. **UNIDENTIFIED owner.** A mile N. of Spooner Station NV, in Sec. 2, T14N R18E. Probable site of at least one waterpowered mill, possibly more. (Koerber.)

131. **UNIDENTIFIED owner.** In Squaw Valley. Op. 1863. Mill probably operated for only a year or so, strictly to supply the shortlived towns of Knoxville and Claraville. They sprang up with a mining boom that aborted when presumed ore bodies proved to be nonexistent. (FC 7-25-1863; USFS p.9.)

132. **UNIDENTIFIED owner.** Lath mill on Brown's Creek NV. 1½ mi. S. of Galena. In W½ of Sec. 14, T17N R19E. Op. 1865–67? (GLO 1865 & 1867 T17N R19E; Ratay.)

133* **UNIDENTIFIED owner.** In Euer Valley prior to 1917. Moved that year by R. Gracey to Deep Creek. (Timberman 8-15-1917.)

133a **UNIDENTIFIED owner.** Mill on Brown's Creek NV. 3 mi. SW of Galena. In NW¼ Sec. 21, T17N R19E. Op. 1867? (Ratay; Koerber.)

133b **UNIDENTIFIED owner.** In Clear Creek NV, in Sec. 4, T14N R18E. (Koerber.)

133c **UNIDENTIFIED owner.** In Clear Creek NV, in Sec. 3, T14N R19E. (Koerber.)

133d **UNIDENTIFIED owner.** On spur of Glenbrook-Spooner RR, in Sec. 3, T14N R18E. Probably was shingle mill. (Koerber.)

133e **UNIDENTIFIED owner.** Adjacent to Secret Harbor of Lake Tahoe in Sec. 23, T15N R18E. Probably two sites. (Koerber.)

133f **UNIDENTIFIED owner.** On Franktown Creek NV in NW¼ Sec. 22, T16N R19E. Waterpowered. (Koerber.)

UNION Mill. *See A. H. Wilson* (142).

134* **VAUGHN, James E.** Shingle mill 6 mi. from Truckee (in Russel Valley?) Op. 1873–? Burned and rebuilt in both 1873 and 1876. Holdings purchased in Feb. 1873 from federal government incl. NW¼ of Sec. 32, T18N R17E. (GHDN 7-11-1873; Nevada.)

VERDI Lumber Co. *See Lonkey* (71).

VERDI Mill Co. Dog Valley Mill. *See Lonkey & Smith* (70).

135* **WAGNER, John, and Jacob Klein.** On Clear Creek NV. Op. 1867–? Hiram Coldwell, a logger, crushed while unloading logs. (CDA 6-26-1867.)

WALLACE. *See Sisson, Wallace & Co.* (110a).

136. **WALLIN.** On Evans Creek NV, in SE¼ of Sec. 7, T18N R19E. Op. 1860? (Kelly 1862; GLO 1867 T18N R19E.)

WARD Bros. *See Porter, Mitchell & Bruhnes* (95).

137* **WARD & FLETCHER.** Crystal Peak Shingle Factory. Located along flume between Dog Valley and Verdi. Op. 1877–? Daily capacity 12–15,000 shingles. (PRP 10-6-1877.)

138. **WARREN, George.** Mill was just downriver from present dam for Stampede Reservoir. Op. 1907. Transported output to Boca over Boca-Loyalton RR. (Jackson p55.)

139* **WATSON, Judge.** Mill near Ophir. Op. 1862. Possibly the J. S. Watson who in 1864 bought ⅙ of a 1,000 acre parcel on the N. shore of Lake Tahoe from Jacob Kelly. (MSP 1-25-1862; Washoe.)

140. **WATSON, R. H.** Mill site ½ mi. N. of mouth of Burton Creek CA. Op. 1927–33. Cut 240 acres, mostly second growth. Watson was evidently a descendant of the J. S. Watson who purchased land in this vicinity from Jacob Kelly in 1864, an acreage that corresponds approximately with that reported cut. (Watson.)

140a* **WEED, Abner.** Fuelwood producer. Headwaters of Sage Hen Creek CA. Op. 1870s–1880s. Moved to Siskiyou County in 1889, where he founded the city of Weed. (Angel p282; Lord p351.)

WELCH. *See Parsons Bros.* (91).

WELLS, FARGO. *See Goff* (38).

WHITBECK, D.D. *See Akin, et al* (1).

WHITE, W. D. *See Eastman & White* (28).

141* **WHITE'S CANYON Flume Co.** In White's Canyon NV. Op. 1876–78. One steampowered saw. (PCBD 1876.)

141a* **WICKS, A. M.** Fuelwood producer. Op. 1870s. Timber ranch of 790 acres near Bronco. (Angel p282; Lord 351.)

WILLIAM. *See John Dixon* (25).

WILLIAMS. *See Caldwell* (13).

142. **WILSON, A. H.** Union Mill. Probably 1 mi. S. of town of Galena NV. Op. 1863–67 by Wilson; 1868 by George Miller & Heaton. (Kelly 63; Wells; Washoe; Koerber.)

WILSON, A. H. *See Alford* (2).

WINTERS, N. D. *See Pray* (96).

143. **WOODBURN, Robert "Old Rob."** A native of Ireland. Mill on Trout Creek 1 mi. S. of Sierra House in Lake Valley, CA. Op. 1860–88. From timber-faced earth-rock dam mill race 10 feet wide carried water through a flume to a small undershot mill wheel. Single up & down saw. Daily cut 6–10,000 ft. Reportedly Yerington & Bliss (through El Dorado Flume & Lumber Co.) bought Woodburn's property in 1887 to get right-of-way for 13 mi. of narrow gauge carrying logs to wharf at Bijou. Once the Woodburn mill served as the Lake Valley post office. There is some question about the location of the Woodburn mill, since one report places the site about 1 mi. W. of the Sierra House (thus possibly on the upper Truckee River, not Trout Cr.). (Angel p380; VC 7-28-1888; Scott; Greuner p13; Hinkle.)

WORN. *See McMillan & Worn* (84).

YERINGTON. *See Spooner* (117).

YERINGTON, H. M. *See Ashe* (4); *Lonkey* (69); *Woodburn* (143).

144. **YERINGTON, H. M., & D. L. Bliss.** Carson & Tahoe Lumber & Flume Co. Two mills were located at Glenbrook, near wharf. #1 (Rigby) mill built in 1873 was N. of #2 and 300 yards S. of Glenbrook Mill Co. It ran until 1897. Mill #2 built in 1875, burned in 1887. Then mill #1 went on 24-hour operation. Capacity, total of both mills, 150,000 ft. daily. Logs in rafts towed by steamers *Emerald* and *Truckee* across lake from Sugar Pine Point and Lake Valley. Mill output went 8.2 mi. by narrow gauge RR up to

Spooners Summit, where it was flumed to Carson City wood terminal. Cordwood carried by barges (180 cords capacity each) across lake. The company cut 80,000 acres and produced a total of 750 million ft of lumber and ½ million cords of fuel wood. Silent partner in N.Y. who with ⅓ interest financed start of operation was D. O. Mills. (GHDN 8-5-1875, 12-10-1875; TE 12-17-1880; NSGR 1890 p188; Scott.)

YERINGTON & Bliss. *See Elliott Bros.* (31); *Pray* (96); *Spooner* (118).

YUBA Mill. *See John Dixon* (25).

Sources Cited

Abbrev.

Adams   Adams, Kramer A. *Logging Railroads of the West*. Seattle: Superior Publishing.

AL   *American Lumberman*.

Angel   Angel, Myron, ed. *History of Nevada*. 680 pp. illus. Oakland: Thompson & West, 1881.

Bancroft   Bancroft, Hubert Howe. *History of Nevada, Colorado and Wyoming*. 827 pp. San Francisco: The History Co., 1890.

BL   Bancroft Library.

Bragg   Bragg, A. O. *Pioneer Days in Nevada*. Second Biennial Report. Reno: Nevada Historical Society, 1911.

Casey   Information provided to author by J. B. Casey of Sparks, NV in 1938.

CBF   California State Board of Forestry. *Biennial Report*. Sacramento: State Printer, 1912.

CIT   *California Illustrated Times*.

CDA   *Carson Daily Appeal*.

Davis   Davis, Sam P. *The History of Nevada*. Reno: Elms Publishing, 1913.

Douglas   Deed Book, Office of Douglas County Recorder, Minden, NV.

EDR   *El Dorado Republican*. Placerville, CA.

Edwards   Edwards, W. F. *Tourists' Guide and Directory of the Truckee Basin*. Truckee: Republican Job Print, 1883.

Fahey   Fahey, John. *The Days of the Hercules*. Moscow, ID: University of Idaho Press, 1978.

FC   *Foresthill Courier*.

GHDN   *Gold Hill Daily News*.

GLO   General Land Office Plats.

Goodwin   Goodwin, Victor O. *Verdi and Dog Valley: A Story of Land Abuse and Restoration*. Elko: U.S. Forest Service Office Report, 1960.

Gracey   Information provided to author by Robert Gracey of Nevada County in 1938.

Gregory   Information provided to author by James Gregory of Washoe in 1938.

Greuner   Greuner, Lorene. *Lake Valley's Past: A Guide to 20 Historic Sites At Tahoe's South Shore*. Mimeographed. South Lake Tahoe: Lake Tahoe Historical Society, 1971.

Grignon   Information provided to author by W. O. Grignon of Verdi in 1938.

Hamlin   Hamlin, John. *Tales of an Old Lumber Camp*. D. C. Heath, 1936.

Hinkle   Hinkle, George and Bliss. *Sierra Nevada Lakes*. Reno: University of Nevada Press, 1987 (Reprint of 1949 edition).

Jackson   Jackson, W. Turrentine. *Historical Survey of the Stampede Reservoir Area in the Little Truckee Drainage District.* San Francisco: National Park Service, USDI, 1967.

James   James, George Wharton. *Lake of the Sky.* Chicago: Charles T. Downer, 1956.

JRP   *History of Tahoe National Forest: 1840-1940.* Davis: Jackson Research Projects, 1982.

Kelly 62   Kelly, J. Wells. *First Directory of Nevada Territory.* San Francisco: Commercial Steam Presses, 1862.

Kelly 63   Kelly, J. Wells. *Second Directory of Nevada Territory.* San Francisco, Valentine, 1863.

Knowles   Knowles, Constance D. *A History of Lumbering in the Truckee Basin from 1856-1936.* Berkeley: Calif. Forest and Range Experiment Station, USFS, 1942.

Koerber   Information provided to author by Arthur Koerber of Incline Village in 1991.

Lardner   Lardner, W. B., and M. J. Brock. *History of Placer and Nevada Counties.* Los Angeles: Historic Record Co., 1924. (Reprinted 1990 by Nevada County Historical Society, Nevada City, CA.)

Lord   Lord, Eliot. *Comstock Mining and Miners.* U.S. Geological Survey Monograph, Washington, D.C., 1883.

MA   *Morning Appeal.* Carson City, NV.

McKeon   McKeon, Owen E. *The Railroads and Steamers of Lake Tahoe.* South Lake Tahoe: Lake Tahoe Historical Society, 1984.

Meschery   Meschery, Joanne. *Truckee, An Illustrated History of the Town and Its Surroundings.* Truckee: Rocking Stone Press, 1978.

Mitchell   Information provided to author by Pat Mitchell of Verdi in 1938.

MM   *The Mountain Messenger.* Downieville, CA.

Mosconi   Information provided to author by Joe Mosconi of Verdi in 1987.

MSP   *Mining and Scientific Press.* San Francisco, CA.

Myrick   Myrick, David. *Railroads of Nevada and Eastern California.* Two volumes. Berkeley: Howell-North Books, 1962.

Nevada   Deed Book, Office of Nevada County Clerk-Recorder, Nevada City, CA.

NSGR   *Nevada Surveyor General Report.* 1890.

NSJ   *Nevada State Journal.*

Ormsby   Deed Book, Office of Ormsby County Recorder, Carson City, NV.

PCBD   *Pacific Coast Business Directory.* San Francisco: Henry G. Langley, 1867, 1871, and 1876.

PCWI   *Pacific Coast Wood and Iron.*

Placer   Deed Book, Office of Placer County Recorder, Auburn, CA.

Porter   Information provided to author by Horace Porter of Washoe County in 1938.

PRP   *Pacific Rural Press.*

Ratay   Ratay, Myra Sauer. Map in *Pioneers of the Ponderosa.* Sparks: Western Printing and Publishing, 1973.

REB   *Reno Evening Bulletin.*

REG   *Reno Evening Gazette.*

RG   *Reno Gazette.*

Richardson Information provided to author by Warren B. Richardson (grandson of mill owner) of Reno in 1987.

Schmidt   Information provided to author by A. Schmidt of Floriston in 1938.

Scott   Scott, E. B. *Saga of Lake Tahoe.* San Francisco: Filmer Bros., 1957.

SFB   *San Francisco Bulletin.*

SFH   *San Francisco Herald.*

Sierra   Deed Book, Office of Sierra County Clerk-Recorder, Downieville, CA.

Smith   Information provided to author by George Smith of Verdi in 1938.

SVL   *Sierra Valley Leader.* Sierraville, CA.

TE   *Daily Territorial Enterprise.* Virginia City, NV.

TNF   Toiyabe National Forest map, ½ inch to 1 mile scale, 1983.

TR   *Truckee Republican.*

TST   *The Truckee Semi-Weekly Tribune.*

TT   *The Timberman.*

USFS   *Cultural and Historical Significance of the Lake Tahoe Region.* A guide for planning. Mimeographed. U.S. Forest Service, 1971.

VC   *Virginia Chronicle.* Virginia City, NV.

Washoe   Deed Book, Office of Washoe County Recorder, Reno, NV.

Watson   Information provided to author by R. H. Watson of Tahoe City in 1938.

WCES   *Washoe City Eastern Slope.*

WCL   *West Coast Lumbermans Directory of Pacific Coast Mills.* 1917.

Wells   Wells, Harry Laurens. *History of Nevada County, California.* Oakland: Thompson & West, 1880.

Wren   Wren, Hon. Thomas. *History of the State of Nevada.* NY: Lewis Publishing, 1904.

Index

Akin, James, 65
Alder Creek, CA, 31, 68, 72, 79
Alder Creek Mill, 31, 72, 77
Alford, Wm. and Rusel, 65, 67
Allen, W., 72, 77
Arnold, D., 65
Arnold, Henry, 75
Ash Creek, NV, 2, 65, 70, 80
Ashe, Alexander, 65-66
Bachelder, J. H., 66-67
Baker, Jesse, 75
Baldwin, Elias Jackson "Lucky," 66
Banner Mill, 74
Barrett, C. R., 11, 66, 77
Barrow, Charles W., 80
Barton, H. C., 50-51
Berg, 78
Best & Belcher Mine, 48
Bijou, CA, 82
Black, 66
Blairsden, CA, 68
Bliss, Charles T., 64
Bliss, Duane L., 9, 39, 40, 49, 50, 63, 66, 77, 79, 82-83
Bliss, William W., 63
Boca, CA, 30, 45, 48, 65, 68, 77, 81
Boca and Loyalton Railroad, 75, 76, 81
Boca Mill and Ice Co., 30, 38, 39, 49, 60, 65
Boni (Boney), Leon, 60, 66
Boston Mill, 73
Bowker, 71
Box factories, 33, 34, 36, 74, 77, 78
Bragg Albert, 6, 30, 49, 66
Bragg, Charles Allen, 6, 27, 30, 49, 66, 72, 77
Brickell, E. J., 27, 28, 30, 34, 66
Brockway, CA, 79
Bronco, CA, 41, 72, 82
Brown, E. D., 77
Brown's Creek, NV, 75, 81
Brown's Mill, 77
Bruhnes, Adolph C., 76-77
Bull donkey engine, 51, 53, 54, 74
Bunker Mill, 66
Burkhalter Mill, 72
Burkhalter Railroad, 72
Burkhart, Charles, 67
Burton Creek, CA, 60, 82
Butler, J., 77
Cable yarding, 51-53
Caldwell, 67
Camp 16, CA, 70, 74
Camp 18, CA, 72, 80
Camp 19, CA, 65, 80
Camp 20, CA, 70
Campbell, 80
Canyon 23-24 Flats, 70
Carriage, log, 14
Carson and Tahoe Lumber and Flume Co., 9, 40, 49, 63, 69, 77, 82
Carson City, NV, 2, 11, 30, 69, 70
Carson Range, 1, 2, 7, 20, 27, 40, 41, 61-62
Carson River, 1
Carson Valley, NV, 1, 11, 15, 43
Casnell, 67
Cattle ranches, 45, 59
Celio, C. G., and Sons, 60, 67
Celio Ranch, CA, 67
Central Mill, 6, 66
Central Pacific Railroad (CPRR), ix, 8, 11, 25, 26, 29, 34, 37, 43, 45, 56, 59, 69, 74-75, 77-78
Chapin, Samuel A., 65, 67
Charcoal, 41, 79
Chedic, Geo. W., 67
Chinese employees, 7, 41, 48, 74, 79
Chubbuck, George Washington, 41
Chutes, 20-25, 37, 53-54
Cisco, CA, 27
Claraville, CA, 81
Clark, 80
Clear Creek, NV, 10, 15, 19, 27, 67, 69, 70, 72, 73, 78, 81
Clear Creek Flume, 15, 18, 19
Clear cutting, 61-62, 74
Clinton, CA, 6, 27, 72
Coburn Station, CA, 27
Cold Creek, CA, 80
Coldstream Creek, CA, 59, 75, 79, 80
Coldwell, Hiram, 9, 81
Colwell, Augustus, 67
Comanche Mill, 76
Comstock, 67
Comstock Silver Lode, ix, 2, 6, 11, 25, 30, 43, 48, 49
Consolidated Virginia & California Mine, 48
Cordwood, 7, 25, 30, 41, 48, 56-57, 74, 79, 82, 83
Coyote Mill, 67
Crown-Columbia Co., 69
Crown-Willamette Co., 59, 69
Crystal Peak, NV, 70, 73, 76-77
Crystal Peak Lumber Co., 39, 67, 70-71
Crystal Peak Shingle Factory, 36, 81-82
Dairy cattle, 45, 59
Davies, 67
Davies, Llewellyn and Sons, 31, 49, 67-68, 72
Davies Sons, 49, 68
Davies Box & Lumber Co., 68
Davis, Charlton, 80
Davis and Son, 70
Deep Creek, CA, 60, 70, 81
Deidesheimer, Philip, 25
Deming, Theo., 79-80
Denio, A., 73
Denton, Reuben, 72
Dimmick, 80
Dixon, John, 68
Dixon, Joseph, 68
Doan, Latimer E., 65
Doan Steam Wagon, 46
Doane, 69, 70
Dog Valley, CA, 27, 39, 46, 51, 68, 70, 73, 74, 76, 78, 81
Dog Valley Mill, 73-74
Dog Valley Summit, 66, 70, 73, 79
Dolbeer donkey engine, 51-53, 73, 74, 76-77
Donkey engines, 20-21, 51-52
Donner Boom & Lumber Co., 37, 41, 68
Donner-Henness Pass Road (see also Henness Pass Turnpike), 70

Donner Lake, CA, 27, 51, 66, 68, 69, 75, 80
Duffy Camp, CA, 59, 69
Dutch Flat, CA, 27, 30, 34, 80
Dyer Mill, 19, 68
Eager, 77
Eagle Mill, 68
Eastman, C. H., 38
Eclipse Mill, 80
Edwards, 78
El Dorado Flume and Lumber Co., 82
Elkhorn Mill, 77
Ellen, Elle, 30, 31, 49, 68-69, 77
Elliott, 73
Elliott Bros. (George, John, Thomas, William), 69
Emery, Joshua, 79-80
Essex Mill, 69, 70
Euer Valley, CA, 70, 81
Evans Creek, NV, 19, 48, 74, 80, 81
Excelsior Mill, 19, 51, 70, 71
Fagan, 68
Fair, James, 19, 20, 48, 49, 71, 74
Fallen Leaf Lake, CA, 67, 69
Fallen Leaf Mill, 69
Ferguson, R. P., 70
Fires, 55-57
Firs, 25, 27, 57, 58
Fishing industry, 45
Flanigan, P. L., 69, 80
Fleischacker Brothers, 59
Fletcher, 36, 81-82
Floriston, CA, 58-59, 66, 69, 70, 79
Floriston Pulp and Paper Co., 58, 69, 70
Flumes, 15-16, 18, 19, 37, 41
Folsom, Gilman N., 6, 27, 30, 49, 66, 72
Forest Mill, 80
Foulkes, John P., 69-70
Foulkes, George, 69-70
Franktown, NV, 1, 6, 27, 48, 66, 72, 73, 76, 80
Franktown Creek, NV, 66, 80, 81
Furniture factory, 34
Gage, Steve, 70

Galena, NV, 48, 65, 72, 75, 76, 77, 81, 82
Galena Creek, NV, 7, 13, 65, 67, 74
Galvin, Dennis, vii
Gardner, M. C., 39
Geisendorfer, George, 29, 30, 66
Gillis, Charles, 15
Gin Pole Loader, 14
Glenbrook, NV, 9, 11, 15, 39, 40, 43, 48, 50, 66, 69, 70, 77, 82
Glenbrook Mill Co., 70, 82
Glenbrook-Spooner Railroad, 81
Glendale, NV, 68, 76
Goff, G. H. F., 70
Goff, J. R., 15
Gold Canyon, NV, 80
Goshen, 70
Gould and Curry Mine, 48
Gracey, Robert G., 60, 67, 81
Graham, J., 69
Gray, Joseph, 27, 70, 78
Gregory, Henry, 2, 65-66, 70, 80
Grey, 71
Haines, J. W., 15
Hale, Horace, 70
Hale and Norcross Mine, 48
Hall (of Larrity & Hall & Revert), 10, 73
Hall (of Martin & Hall), 14, 74-75
Hamlin, S. A., 69, 70-71
Hammond Ranch, 73
Harbin, Matt & Co., 77
Hardy, Kathy, vii
Haskell, 71
Haskell, Wm., 75
Hattery, A., 65
Hawthorne, William A., 2, 71
Hawthorne Mill, 80
Hawthorne Station, 2
Haynie, J. W., 19, 73
Heaton, 76, 82
Henness Pass Turnpike (see also Donner-Henness Pass Road), 76
Henry, Patrick, 39, 70
Higgins, 71
Hilton, F. D., 79
Hirschdale, CA, 57, 72

Hoag, J. V., 69
Hobart, Walter S., 19, 41, 49, 50, 51, 64, 71-72
Hobart Mills, CA, 31, 34-36, 47, 50, 51, 53, 54, 55, 59, 60, 61, 69, 71, 75
Hobart's Ravine, NV, 71
Howe, 71
Horses, 11, 22-24, 37, 51, 52
Huffaker, NV, 20, 48, 74
Hughes, F. J., 72
Hunter Canyon, NV, 69
Hunter Creek, NV, 19, 48, 69, 71, 74, 80
Hunter Lake, NV, 74
Hyde, Orson, 1, 2, 72
Hymer, Thomas K., 72
Ice, 45
Incline, NV, 41, 43, 48, 51, 71
Incline Mill, 41, 43, 71
Ingraham Station, CA, 70, 76
Jackman, William, 60, 66
Jones, Charles, 72
Jones, Thomas R., 72
Jones Valley, CA, 67
Jordan Station, CA, 76
Judah, Theodore, 25
Juniper Creek, CA, 72
Katz, Frederick, 39, 70
Kelly, Jacob, 82
Kidder Bros., 72
King, Samuel, 75
Kings Canyon, NV, 11, 72
King's Ranch, CA, 75
Klein, Jacob, 9, 81
Kneeland, John, 80
Knox, J. R., 15, 72-73
Knoxville, CA, 81
Krisher, H., 68
Kruger, W. H., 27-30, 34, 66
Lake Bigler Lumber Company, 11, 77
Lake Tahoe, 11, 13, 15, 25, 37, 39, 40, 45, 50, 71, 77, 78, 81, 83
Lake Valley, CA, 2, 39, 41, 80, 82, 82
Lakeside, 41
Lakeview, NV, 41, 71, 72, 73
Lapham, William W., 41
Lapham's Hotel and Landing, 41

Larrity, 10, 73
Lawrence, 73
Lawton Hot Springs, NV, 80
Leach, 75
Leavitt, Ben H., 73
Lebroke, Thomas, 73
Lent, Richard, 37
Leonard, Hobart, viii
Lewers, 73
Lewers Creek, NV, 73
Lewis, 73
Lewison, J. L., 79
Lilly, L., 73
Little Bangor, NV, 6, 66
Little Truckee River, CA, 38, 39, 65, 71, 72, 75, 79
Little Valley, NV, 19, 68, 71, 73, 76, 77
Locke, John, 73
Locomotives: Baldwin, 54; Climax 54; *San Mateo*, 27; Shay, 54; at Hobart Mills, 55, 57
Log rails, 44
Lonkey, John, 73
Lonkey, Oliver, 14, 15, 27, 29, 30, 33, 49, 73-75
Loomis, George, 74
Lynham Camp, 70
Macauley, Thomas, vii
Machomick, James, 31, 77
Mackay, John, 19, 20, 48, 49, 71, 74
Marker, Hans and Peter, 6, 7, 74
Marlette, Samuel H., 19, 41, 49, 50, 51, 64, 71-72
Marlette Lake, NV, 19
Marlick, 77
Martin, 75
Martin, S. B., 67
Martin, Seth, 14, 70, 74-75
Martis Creek, CA, 71, 75, 77-78
Martis Valley, CA, 68, 78
Marysville Mill
Mason, 72
Mayflower Mill, 77
McFarland, Samuel, 75
McGiffert Loader, 13
McIntosh, Alexander, 70-71
McKay, Stewart, 29, 75
McKinney Creek, CA, 67
McMillan, 75
McPherson, Angus, 75

Meacham, R. S., 70-71
Meadow Lake, CA, 73
Merrill, George, 70
Merrill Creek, CA, 73, 77
Merrill Valley, CA, 67
Merrill Valley Lumber Co., CA, 67
Meyers Station, CA, 60, 67
Mill City, NV, 48, 71
Mill Creek, NV, 2, 65, 70, 71, 80
Mill ponds, 45
Miller, 76
Miller, Andrew H., 79
Miller, George, 82
Mills, D. O., 83
Milne, D. B., 67
Mitchel, Charles, 68
Mitchell, 76-77
Monitor Mill, 72
Montrose, 73
Morton, 76
Mosconi, Joe, viii
Mount Rose, 62
Mules, 7
Munger, 76
Murdock, 11
Musgrove, W. R., 76
Negus, T. G., 73
Nevada and California Lumber Co., 74-75
Nevada Ice Co., 70
New York Mill, 77
Nichols, H. O., 76
Norcross, Thomas, 76
Oliver, George D., 64
Ophir, NV, 27, 33, 48, 73, 76, 81
Ophir Mill Co., 6, 76
Overton, J. B., 51, 64
Oxen, 11, 12, 22, 37, 51
Pacific Shingle Co., 70
Pacific Wood and Lumber Co., 30, 49, 57, 72
Pacific Wood, Lumber & Flume Co., 19, 48, 74
Parker Claim, 73
Parks, D., 69
Parsons, Nathan and Jay, 76
Patton, "Red," 73
Perkins Ranch, 73
Person, Acey (or Asa), 7, 65, 76
Pine, CA, 76
Pines, xiv, 25, 27, 57

Placerville, CA, 1
Planing mills, 33, 36, 74
Poor, J. J., 71
Porter, 76-77
Pray, A. W., 11, 77
Preempted lands, 26
Price, Wm. E., 77
Price Lake, NV, 77
Price's Mill, 19
Prince, Thomas B., 77
Proctor, A., 77
Proctor, Alexander and Daniel, 77
Prosser Creek, CA, 14, 70, 72, 74, 75
Prosser Creek Station, CA, 74
Pulp mills, 58-59
Railroads, 8, 9, 11, 15, 25-27, 29, 30, 34, 37, 37, 43, 44, 45, 49, 50, 54, 55, 59, 66, 69, 70, 72, 74-79, 82-83
Ralston, 73
Ramsey, 13, 65
Ramsey Mill, 65
Reed, 77
Reno, NV, 19, 20, 30, 38
Reservoirs, 37, 45
Revert, Al, 10, 73
Richardson, Warren and George, 30, 41, 44, 45, 46, 69, 77-78
Riddle, James, 2, 66, 80
Rideout, J. R., 65
Rideout, N., 65
Rigby, James H., 72
Rigby Mill, 82
River driving, 37-39, 72
Robinson, John, 68
Roberson, Charles E., 31, 77
Rose, Jacob, 1, 72
Russel Valley, CA, 79, 81
Sage Hen Creek, CA, 41, 74, 79, 82
Salt Lake City, UT, 1
Samson, 78
Sardine House, CA, 76
Sardine Valley, CA, 67-68, 75, 76
Sash and door factories, 34, 36, 74
Saws: band, 14, 33, 54; chain, 37; circular, 5, 14; crosscut, 37; upright, 3, 14

Saxton, Augustus H. and Reuben H., 13, 78
Schock, Caspar, 78
Scofield, N. E., 79
Sears, Wm. R., 67
Secret Harbor, NV, 81
Shaffer, George H., 27, 29, 30, 49, 77, 78-79
Shake makers, 36
Sherman, C. P., 80
Sherrick, James, 9-10, 73
Sherritt, James, 79
Shingle mills, 36, 70, 72, 78, 79, 80, 81
Sides, R. D., 2, 72
Sierra House, NV, 41, 80-81, 82
Sierra Nevada Wood and Lumber Co., 34, 41-43, 49, 50, 64, 71, 79
Sierra Valley, CA, 50
Silver State Mill, 80
Simonds, S. H., 66
Sinkers, 38
Sisson, Wallace and Co., 41, 75, 78, 79
Skidding logs, 21-22, 37, 51, 54, 60
Slack, Wm. A., 76
Slide Mountain, NV, 19, 77
Smith, 49
Smith, David G., 59, 79
Smith, E. R., 14, 73-75
Smith, I. A., 79
Snodgrass, John, 73, 79
Snowsheds, 25
Snug Saloon, 69
Southern, B. S., 73
Splash dams, 37, 68
Spool post, 20
Spooner, Michele E., 73, 79
Spooner Station, NV, 15, 17, 40, 79, 81
Spooner Summit, NV, 49, 73
Sproul, 70
Sproul, R., 79-80
Square sets, 48
Squaw Valley, CA, 78, 81
Stage, 73
Stampede Reservoir, 81
Stanford, A. P., 80
Stanford Station, CA, 69, 79
Star, CA, 75

Starbuck, 76
Stateline Mill, 70
Steamboat Springs, NV, 77
Steamboats, 11, 41, 71, 82
Steam power, 5, 13, 14, 54
Steam wagons, 41, 44, 46, 47, 73
Steele, Wm. R., 68
Stevens, W. F., 80
Stewart, J. A., 29, 75
Stiltz, George, 65
Stiltz, Ramsey and Co., 13
Stockham, 80
Stockman's Mill, 65
Stonewall Station, CA, 80
Sugar Pine Point, CA, 39, 67, 67, 82
Summit Mill, 69, 78
Summit Valley, CA, 77
Sunrise Mill, 76-77
Sweeney, 70, 75
Tahoe City, CA, 48, 50
Tahoe Railroad, 70
Tahoe Tavern, 64
Tailor Creek, CA, 73
Tallac, CA, 73
Thomas, 80
Thomas Canyon, NV, 67, 72, 80
Thompson, 80
Thompson, James M., 70, 80
Thompson, Jesse, 70
Towle Brothers, 27, 80
Tractor logging, 60
Tramlines, 41, 43, 69, 71
Treadwell, Leonard L., 70, 80
Trout Creek, CA, 69, 80, 82
Truckee, CA, 11, 26, 29, 34, 37, 41, 44, 45, 48, 49, 50, 64
Truckee Lumber Co., 28-30, 34, 37, 39, 50, 51, 57, 60, 66, 69, 70-71, 74
Truckee Meadows, 19
Union Mill, NV, 82
Union Mills, CA, 75
Union Valley, CA, 75
Utah Mine, 48
Vaughn, James E., 81
Verdi, NV, 27, 33, 45, 46, 48, 60, 66, 69-71, 74, 81
Verdi Lumber Co., 30, 32-33, 51, 54, 60, 73, 74

Verdi Mill Co., 46, 73-74
Virginia City, NV, 2, 7, 25, 30, 41, 74, 79
Virginia and Truckee Railroad (V&TRR), 30, 41, 49, 57, 71, 74
Wagner, John, 9, 81
Walker Lake, NV, 2
Wallace, 41, 75, 78, 79
Wallin, 81
Walton, 11
Walton, Joseph, 68
Ward, 36, 81-82
Ward, O. M. and Bros., 77
Ward Creek, CA, 50, 78
Warren, 11
Warren, George, 81
Washoe City, NV, 68, 74, 76, 80
Washoe Lake, NV, 6
Washoe Valley, NV, 1, 2, 6, 7, 11, 19
Water power, 3, 13, 14
Watson, J. S., 81
Watson, Judge, 81-82
Watson, R. H., 82
Watson Claim, 73
Watson's Mill, 60
Webber Canyon, CA, 73
Webber Creek, CA, 76
Webber Lake, CA, 71, 73
Weed, Abner, 41, 82
Welch, 76
Wells, Fargo, 70
Whitbeck, D. D., 65
White, W. D., 38, 68
White's Canyon, NV, 74, 82
White's Canyon Flume Co., 82
Wicks, A. M., 41, 82
Willamette donkey engine, 53, 72
William, 68
Williams, 67
Wilson, A. H., 65
Winters, N. D., 11, 77
Winter's Creek, NV, 76
Woodburn, Robert, 82
Woodburn Mill, 77, 80
Woodward, 73
Worn, 75
Yerington, H. M., 9, 39, 40, 48, 49, 50, 63, 66, 66, 73, 77, 79, 82-83
Yuba Mill, 68